INTERROGATING HETERONORMATIVITY IN PRIMARY SCHOOLS:

THE WORK OF THE *NO OUTSIDERS* PROJECT

INTERROGATING HETERONORMATIVITY IN PRIMARY SCHOOLS:
THE WORK OF THE *NO OUTSIDERS* PROJECT

edited by
Renée DePalma and Elizabeth Atkinson

Trentham Books
Stoke on Trent, UK and Sterling. USA

Trentham Books Limited
Westview House   22883 Quicksilver Drive
734 London Road   Sterling
Oakhill   VA 20166-2012
Stoke on Trent   USA
Staffordshire
England ST4 5NP

© 2009 Renée DePalma and Elizabeth Atkinson

First published 2009

British Library Cataloguing-in-Publication Data
A catalogue record for this book is available from the British Library

Cover photo by David Williams

ISBN: 978 1 85856 458 6

Designed and typeset by Trentham Print Design Ltd, Chester and printed in Great Britain by Cromwell Press Group, Trowbridge

Contents

Introduction

Renée DePalma and Elizabeth Atkinson

From September 2006 to December 2008[1], members of the *No Outsiders* research team explored ways in which heteronormativity operates in primary schools and classrooms. Our goal was to interrupt these processes. The project took its name from a statement made by Archbishop Desmond Tutu in the context of the heated debate over homosexuality within the Anglican church community. Tutu proclaimed, 'Everyone is an insider, there are no outsiders – whatever their beliefs, whatever their colour, gender or sexuality' (25 February 2004). The title of the project is deliberately ambivalent. On one hand, it echoes Archbishop Tutu's insistence that there are no outsiders, while on the other, it reminds us that the effect of normalisation, whether in relation to race, class, gender, disability, sexuality or other features of identity, is to convey to outsiders that they have no place in 'our' society: a message conveyed not only by explicit acts of discrimination but also by simply doing nothing. The *No Outsiders* project aimed to support teachers in challenging that message within their own schools.

Directed by Elizabeth Atkinson and Renée DePalma, the project was funded by the Economic and Social Research Council (ESRC, RES-062-23-0095) to permit collaboration of the University of Sunderland with the University of Exeter, the Institute of Education (University of London) and 15 primary schools across England. By the second year of the project, it had expanded to include a total of over 40 participants at 16 sites, including a nursery and a local authority.

Over the nearly three-year lifespan of the project, beginning with interviewing university researchers and contacting potential schools in Spring 2006, through the school-based inquiry to the final editing of this book in the Spring of 2009, the project has grown, shifted and complexified in ways we could not have imagined when we wrote the initial funding bid. Yet this very unpredictability is in a way what we expected and hoped for. Drawing upon a methodological framework of Participatory Action Research (PAR, described in detail in Chapter 8), we insisted from the beginning that research would be designed according to an ecological perspective, based on local realities and practices and the particular interests of team members. This perspective also meant that we as researchers would consider ourselves as part of the system we were studying.

We started with the following broad general research objectives:

- to add to the understanding of the operation of heteronormativity – the normalisation of heterosexuality to the exclusion of any other identities – in school contexts

- to develop effective means of challenging this heteronormativity

- to create a community of practice within which teachers can develop effective approaches to addressing sexualities equality within the broader context of inclusive education

- to enhance teacher professional development and autonomy through action and critical reflection

The team collated a resource pack drawn from existing published materials, including videos, posters and books depicting gay and lesbian characters, same-sex parents and non-gender conforming protagonists. Whole-school training was provided by the project diversity trainer (Mark Jennett) and the project also funded performers, artists, workshops facilitators and documentary film-makers. In collaboration with university researchers, teacher researchers developed specific areas of investigation arising from their own interests and interrogations of everyday practice. This has by no means been a straightforward process, and it is the inherent tensions and complexities that we discovered along the way that are explored in this book. Over the course of the project we figured out how to articulate the questions that we, as a team, were trying to answer. Taken as a whole across the entire project team, these areas of focus can be summarised in the following questions:

- How can sexual orientation be addressed for children in ways that are relevant to their experience and growing understanding of personal identity, love and family diversity?

- How can this work be extended across and beyond the curriculum?

- Can literature and the creative and performing arts be particularly powerful in drawing upon the imagination to help broaden understandings and shift attitudes?

- How does transgender equality relate to gender equality, and how might gender equality work in primary schools go beyond challenging a 'blue for boys, pink for girls' discourse to question gender binaries?

- What kinds of preparatory work are helpful, in terms of staff and administration as well as parents and community?

- How can parents' concerns be addressed, both proactively and as they arise?

- How can coalition-building be developed between marginalised groups who may not previously have seen each other as allies?

- How can teachers' own sexual identities and gender expression support or constrain sexualities equality work in the classroom?

- How can sexualities equality be incorporated into the values and ethos of a Church school, and into the inclusive tenets of Islam?

- How might lesbian and gay teachers act as role models for pupils?

- How might queer theory inform classroom practice?

Practice at each research site was designed as part of and in response to these lines of inquiry. Defining these particular questions was an important part of the research, and we have collected project teachers' responses to them in another volume, entitled *Undoing Homophobia in Primary Schools*, also to be published by Trentham. Underlying these questions, however, we began to explore deeper lines of inquiry, related to subtler and less tangible themes: themes of silence and speaking out, faith and culture, leadership and role-modelling, personal and emotional investment, gay rights/liberal humanist and queer perspectives, safety and risk-taking, the possibility (or otherwise) of a queer pedagogy, and intersections between (queer) theory and practice. These are the themes which we explore in detail in the present volume.

in the opening chapter the editors reflect on the fundamental tension between the power of destabilisation offered by queer theory and the emancipatory promise of strategic identity-based critical pedagogy. Cullen explores the potential for a queer praxis within the spaces of school, specifically analysing how teachers engaged with different kinds of activism and theory. Youdell considers the relationship between the various conceptual tools, political modes and political goals taken up within and beyond the project in terms of public and media representation.

Nixon, too, examines ways in which the project work has been taken up in public representation. He applies a geographic perspective on safe, troubled and dangerous spaces, and considers what may be lost in embracing safe – what he calls 'vanilla' – practice in potentially dangerous contexts. Allan *et al* also take a geographical perspective, analysing what can happen when the formerly unspeakable is finally spoken within the carefully bounded spaces of schools. Talburt focuses on school and its implicit discourses of futurity and the Child, and questions whether these spaces are so fundamentally un-queer as to preclude the possibility of a 'queer pedagogy.'

Atkinson and Moffat take up the theme of identity politics and queer destabilisations of identity that has run throughout the project, in a more personal exploration of ways in which they have experienced and managed the deployment of their own lesbian and gay identities within and beyond their project work, as a university researcher and teacher researcher respectively. DePalma and Teague also analyse how project members' own sexualities came to fall within the research gaze of the project, focusing on how researchers and teachers came to negotiate the terms of power within this 'democratic community of practice.' Brace explores how the community of practice model has provided opportunities to transform practice, both our own and that of others, through sometimes difficult border negotiations with other practice communities.

Throughout the book, the project members, teachers and university researchers are consistently referred to by our first names, even when our words and actions are being considered as project data and we are in the position of research subjects. We have chosen not to use pseudonyms because we understand that, as members of a collaborative research team, we are all researchers and research subjects alike. Some of the people and organisations who have collaborated with us (for example, Jay Stewart from Gendered Intelligence (www.gendered intelligence.co.uk) have also chosen to be identified by their real names. We have drawn heavily for data not only on our personal research journals, field notes and transcripts of interviews, but also on our email correspondence and the crucial ongoing discussions we have had throughout the project on the discussion forum within the team-members' section of the project website: a forum in which key issues arising within the project were teased out, explored and analysed. Excerpts from these discussions are occasionally lightly edited for grammar and spelling, but we have attempted to keep as much of the original conversational style as possible.

This dialogic process throughout the project has been crucial to deepening our understandings of the project work and developing the multiple perspectives collected as chapters here. If it is true that we have all been subjects of this research, it is also true that we have all been co-researchers and co-authors of the research publications that have come out of the project. We would like to thank all the members of the *No Outsiders* research team, those who are officially recognised here as authors and also those whose contributions are not officially credited with authorship, but which are no less valuable.

Note

1   The project was originally funded for 28 months to December 2008, although it received a 3-month administrative extension to March 2009. The project's work has continued since the end of the funding period, but the focus of this book is on the work which took place up to December 2008.

1

Putting queer into practice: problems and possibilities

Renée DePalma and Elizabeth Atkinson

This chapter explores a theme which recurs in different forms throughout this book: the tension between the destabilisation of norms offered by queer theory and the consciousness-raising and potential emancipation offered by identity politics and related practice. Looking first at the comparative safety offered by recourse to new government requirements and guidelines in carrying out sexualities equality work, the authors go on to examine the possibility of moving beyond these neoliberal discourses and to ask what might constitute a queer practice. Recognising the heterogeneity within the project team and the importance of acknowledging different stances and motivations among the team members, the authors demonstrate how this heterogeneity was played out through the mobilisation of a range of different discourses and practices during the course of the project. They consider what needs to be unlearned if a real unsettling of sex and gender binaries is to be achieved.

Introduction

In the *No Outsiders* project, we have explored how gender, sex and sexuality are conflated in the process of constructing 'appropriate' gendered behaviours and preferences for boys and girls, so that sexism, homophobia and transphobia are all deployed in the policing of heteronormativity (DePalma and Atkinson, 2007a). While at times we have focused separately on gender identity (DePalma, 2009) and sexuality (DePalma and Atkinson, 2009), queer theory, with its emphasis on destabilising categories of sex, gender and sexuality, permits a more complex interrogation of how sex, gender and sexuality intertwine in heteronormative processes.[2]

As project designers, we envisioned the *No Outsiders* project as an alternative to the discourse of victimisation and tolerance underlying traditional UK-based anti-homophobia efforts (DePalma and Atkinson, in press). We sought to answer the question, 'What would it take to teach queerly?' We set out not only to interrogate the heteronormativity implicit in schools but to explore how these processes might be interrupted through critical pedagogical practices.

During the course of the project we developed a more complex understanding of the tensions between queer interrogations and classroom teaching, between queer uncertainties and emancipatory practice. In this chapter we explore these productive tensions. On one hand, we examine the essentialising risks of an identity-based project: what (hetero)sexist stereotypes might be propagated by role-model approaches based on lesbian, gay, bisexual and transgender (LGBT) identity politics? On the other hand, we examine the possibilities afforded by strategically deployed identity work: in what circumstances can identity politics be useful, and who might be harmed by an insistence on fluidity and non-unitary identities?

The comfort and support of government guidance and the (neoliberal) ideological strings attached

The increasing concern with homophobic bullying in schools in the UK and abroad indicates a readiness to recognise sexualities equality, yet government policy and guidance tends to reduce this to an anti-homophobia and anti-transphobia – and more explicitly, a general anti-bullying – stance (Department for Children Schools and Families, 2007; Department for Education and Skills, 2002; Department for Education and Skills and Department of Health, 2004; Home Office, 2008), a discourse we all tend to appropriate when we communicate with government bodies or with the general public through the popular media. While it has not necessarily been our aim to *meet* government requirements in this work, it gives our project teachers added confidence and security to know that what they are doing supports them in meeting their statutory obligations. Such a position has been eloquently summarised by Alan Luke (2006), who identified the role of the critical educational researcher and activist as finding the spaces in policy and policy-making in which critical work can be done.

Nevertheless, government support can be something of a double-edged sword. As Ellis writes in his critique of *Stand up for Us: Challenging homophobia in schools* (Department for Education and Skills and Department of Health, 2004), the careful editing and 'low-key' release of this document contribute to an overall discourse of (silent) tolerance:

> Stand up for us is a plea for tolerance that just doesn't even speak about what is to be tolerated never mind trying to develop teachers' and students' understandings of how heteronormativity or compulsory heterosexuality creates the very conditions in which homophobia is produced. (Ellis, 2007: 21)

In this sense, we recognise that by helping teachers to cast their *No Outsiders* project work in terms of the existing government guidelines we may be offering them the security to engage in professionally risky, ground-breaking equalities work (DePalma, 2009), but that this may in itself steer teachers away from work which might go beyond the scope of neoliberal discourses of equality and tolerance.

Teaching for equality or teaching queerly?

As project members we have also discovered that the stances we take and the discourses we draw upon depend not only on the context and audience but also on our own fundamental understandings of what it means to go beyond tolerance of LGBT people.

Within the project team, we share the conviction that the *status quo*, where the ever-present threat of bullying and exclusion on the basis of perceived sexuality and non-gender normative behaviours results in silences and invisibility, is unacceptable. This kind of 'don't ask, don't tell' tolerance only serves to perpetuate stereotypes and propagate assumptions that all teachers and parents are heterosexual and fit neatly and permanently into existing gender categories. In this sense, we share the view that primary teachers must go beyond an anti-bullying discourse of tolerance in the form of quiet acceptance (in other words, simple lack of overt oppression). We share the view, which is not necessarily expressed in all anti-bullying discourses around homophobia and transphobia, that teachers need to reach beyond passive and disingenuous tolerance of 'those LGBT people' to proactively incorporate discussions of sexuality and gender into their curriculum. We do not, however, agree on how this should be done. Whether tolerant silences and invisibilities can best be disrupted by highlighting lesbian and gay histories and attacking hetero-gender stereotypes or by troubling the binaries implicit in the very categories of lesbian/gay, boy/girl is a question that remains alive and unresolvable in our research.

Drawing upon Wenger and Lave's insistence that a community of practice thrives on heterogeneity and is based on the assumption 'that members have different interests, make diverse contributions to activity, and hold varied viewpoints' (Lave and Wenger, 1991:97), we purposefully set out to design a Participatory Action Research (PAR) community which acknowledged dissensus, rather than consensus, as the starting-point for action (see Chapter 8). We chose not to resolve differences through compromise in ways that would inevitably minimise or silence less powerful voices, and we have aimed to allow the 'tension inherent in the very dynamics of language and the dynamism demanded of the continuous action and reflection, action and reflection, of genuine praxis' (Winkelmann, 1991:4) to persist. Keeping this heteroglossic dialogue (Bakhtin, 1999) alive has constituted an ongoing methodological challenge.

There has been an ongoing debate within the project about the extent to which the use of project books depicting same-sex couples and of gay role models in the form of teachers' own lives might lead to strategies which reinforce essentialist binaries (gay/straight, male/ female). It is important to point out that these approaches tend to privilege some sexualities over others (bisexuality, for example, is not represented in children's literature). In our case, these approaches also privileged traditional (binary) gender experience, since none of our teachers identify as trans or gender-queer, and children's books that deal with gender non-conformity do little to unsettle gender categories as such. However, the project did enlist a consultant to engage project members and some children in exploring gender from a trans perspective, and he explicitly drew upon his own trans experience as part of this work (see DePalma, 2009, for more details).

While some in the project have argued that this kind of identity work implicitly reinforces discourses of victimisation and tolerance (see Rasmussen, 2001; Talburt and Steinberg, 2000 for similar arguments), others have made strong cases for more equalities-based strategic essentialism (see Guha and Spivak, 1988), drawing consciously upon essentialist categories of gay and straight as a way to render transgressive sex and gender identities less exotic and threatening (see Chapter 2, Chapter 7 for further analysis of these perspectives).

There has been an extensive discussion among members of the project team about the nature of queering and whether/to what extent what teachers are doing in classrooms is or can be queer. When Elizabeth (co-author of this chapter and project director) encouraged Andy (teacher researcher) to move away from fixed identity categories in the introduction to an early years teaching resource that he'd written, Andy posted these comments to the website and began a debate around them. First, he posted an excerpt from an email sent to him by Elizabeth:

> I think the key is to strike a balance between keeping things clear-cut and simple ... and being clear that life isn't actually that simple – that sexual identity is a fluid and changing thing, at least for some people ... It's not necessarily about being confused, but simply about variability in relationships and identities.

Then Andy posted his own perspective:

> I have to say I don't really agree with your comments with regard to variability in relationships and identities. While I am aware that I might be putting children into boxes, I think it's important to give children something to identify with if they feel different. By saying 'sexuality is fluid...' aren't you supporting the theory that we all choose and we can be straight if we try?

In contrast, for Laura, another teacher researcher, claiming the label 'gay' felt like a constraint rather than an activist liberation. In response to Andy, she wrote:

> I take the point about when you're different, wanting something to identify with to somehow give some legitimacy and explanation for your difference. And ... when I came out ... I hated the feeling I had to put myself in a box, that I had to put a definitive label on myself. Some queer (for want of a better word) educating at some point in my school life might have helped a bit.

Fin, a university researcher, joined the conversation with the following comment:

> I think for many of the reasons, gendered and sexual essentialism can trouble me – although I understand how powerful it can be as a tool in identity recognition. However, I do recognise that certainties can be easier to communicate...

As this excerpt from a web discussion demonstrates, project members differed in whether they saw themselves as taking a queer perspective as exemplified by Elizabeth's emphasis on fluid sexualities or taking on an approach of strategic essentialism, as exemplified by Andy's 'giving children something to identify with'. Many of us began to examine our own contradictions and inconsistencies in the course of these discussions. Andy later reflected:

> I've been thinking all morning about our discussion re identity and I can see where you are coming from. I talked to a colleague who said I was clearly only interested in pushing 'my gay agenda' (!) which I thought was a bit harsh – but it really made me think about what agenda I am pushing. I always say 'You're gay or you're straight and that's it', but actually I should be saying so much more.

This excerpt is included here not to demonstrate that Andy has changed his mind but to illustrate the process by which he has complicated his own perspective – a process that has been shared by many of us during the course of the project. Neither was Deb, a university researcher, equivocating her strong queer theory perspective when she wrote:

> What's important to me is *queer practice*, practices that trouble hetero/homo binaries, practices ... So for me Queer isn't about an identity, although it is the one I feel most comfortable with, but I'm often also strategically a lesbian...

Identity politics and deconstruction of categories might make uneasy companions, but as Deb points out, many of us are at least occasionally strategically something. Some of us, as Butler puts it, are still highly invested in making sure our strategic essentialism doesn't collapse into just essentialism:

> Identity categories tend to be the instruments of regulatory regimes, whether as the normalising categories of oppressive structures or as the rallying points of a liberatory contestation of that very oppression. This is not to say

> that I will not appear at political occasions under the sign of lesbian, but I would like to have it permanently unclear what precisely that sign signifies. (Butler, 1991:16-17)

Laura points out that it is hard to act from a place of deconstruction, and describes herself as perpetually balanced between queering and acting, as long as strategic essentialism is a temporary position:

> I guess that's partly how one can say [they] can fit together in the under-standing that the action taken is never the end, is never final, can be tried again differently etc ... activism tends to fix identities and concepts, again in a way that is often necessary, but also limiting. It's tricky. Maybe strategic essentialism is the only way to move things forward.

Queering or conforming to the (patriarchal, heterosexist) institution of marriage?

Andy deliberately came out to his pupils just before his civil partnership in the hope that by extending the ways in which the marriages of heterosexual people are celebrated and discussed in primary schools, he could help make gay relationships part of the everyday fabric of school life:

> [My colleagues] will ask about [my partner] in front of people, it's about being out and talking with people just like heterosexual people talk about their weekend with their wives and their girlfriends.

Just before he celebrated his own civil partnership, Miles, a head teacher, held an assembly for year 4 and 5 classes in his school. He con-nected his own upcoming celebration with a reading of the book *King and King* (de Haan and Nijland, 2000), a story of two princes who fall in love:

> I started by reading *King and King* which some of the children were familiar with. At the end of the book I commented there was a similarity for me as I would be marrying my partner who was male in the half term holiday ... During lunchtime many children congratulated me and wished me well. At the end of the day a group of girls came to my room with some cards they had made for [us]. A parent and her three children also came with a card and a bottle of wine as she was 'just so pleased and wanted you to know how great we think it is'.

7

These vignettes illustrate Andy's and Miles' attempts to disrupt the heteronormative processes that have systematically denied lesbians and gay men privileges usually reserved for heterosexuals. Not only do they claim their right to have their partnerships recognised in law, recently conferred by the UK government via the Civil Partnership Act (brought into force in December, 2005), but by doing this in the space of a public primary school they insist that their privilege become normalised (in the form of the everyday naming of Andy's partner and of Miles' celebratory cards and wine).

Nevertheless, such normalising processes have not been uncritically accepted by everyone in the project. Annie, who identifies as a straight woman, has drawn upon a feminist perspective to critique the very institution of marriage that some lesbian and gay activists have been fighting to be included in:

> I never got married, I am a feminist ... yet all these gay people around me are rushing into civil ceremonies and these fancy weddings. And there is a part of me that wants to go excuse me, excuse me, do you know what a wedding is all about, it's about property. I didn't want my father to walk me down the aisle and give me away to another man as a virgin.

As Charpentier (n.d.) points out, the words 'I pronounce you man and wife' as a performative speech act is disrupted (or is it perhaps reinforced?) by the impossibility of 'I pronounce you man and man' or 'I pronounce you wife and wife'. The question is whether same-sex couples' appropriation of traditionally straight weddings (including, in some cases, the word itself, despite the fact that they are only legally entitled to a civil partnership) queers or reinforces the patriarchal and heterosexist institution of marriage.

Are gay penguins queer?

Each school participating in the *No Outsiders* project received a set of resources including a range of storybooks depicting lesbian, gay and non-gender conforming characters. For many teachers, simply having these books in the school has made a significant impact. As our earlier research suggests (DePalma and Atkinson, 2006, 2007b, 2009; Atkinson and DePalma, 2008a), the silence around sexualities in general in primary schools is a powerful force which renders problematic any attempt to break it. A book about two people who fall in love, two penguins raising a chick or a teenage boy deciding whether and how to 'fit in' can become a dangerous presence if the two people both happen to be princes, the two penguins both happen to be male and the teenage boy happens to be gay. In the UK it was a book about a small girl, her daddy and his (male) partner that instigated Section 28 of the 1988 Local Government Act which, despite its repeal in England in 2003, was still cited by some of our earlier research participants as a deterrent to even mentioning gay and lesbian identities in the class-room (Section 28 of the 1988 Local Government Act stated that a local authority shall not 'promote the teaching in any maintained school of the acceptability of homosexuality as a pretended family relationship'). In this climate, simply opening the box containing the project books in the staffroom became a risky political act.

Nevertheless, there has been an on-going debate among the project team around the danger of reinscribing certain social norms, such as monogamy and child-bearing, through books that portray gay and lesbian characters within these normative families, such as *And Tango Makes Three* (Parnell *et al*, 2005): a particularly well-loved project book telling the true story of two male penguins who raise a chick together. Laura raised the concern in the web discussion:

> I'm really concerned about the ways in which I find myself latching on to knowable safe images of gay daddies and lesbian mummies or at least gay and lesbian couples falling in love. I guess I'm partly led to this safe, middle of the road place by the project books which inscribe these notions of romantic, monogamous relationships (albeit with gay people or penguins rather than straight ones).

Andy, however, rejected the notion that we need move beyond gay penguins:

> I just like the fact that we are talking about gay penguins. I don't think we need to get beyond that at this stage. We are in the early stages of this nationally, this sort of thought process. The fact that we've got gay penguins is fantastic, why do we need to worry about what's next? We need to get schools to do, to talk about gay penguins because at the moment ... most schools aren't doing anything.

The debate over whether or not we need to 'move beyond gay penguins' is one manifestation of the tension between strategic essentialist and queer approaches that runs throughout the project. As Andy argues, children need to recognise the category 'gay' in order to undo a socially constructed incommensurability between the category of 'gay' and the category of 'loving parents' usually reserved for straight people, an argument we have made in more detail elsewhere (Atkinson and De-Palma, 2009). As Laura argues, however, this essentialism, however strategic, runs the risk of reifying categories that a queer project seeks to disrupt – for example, by reinforcing the perceived superiority of the particular type of monogamous, child-centred family relationship embodied by the penguins. Klara, a visitor to the project from Stockholm, felt that the emphasis on safety restrained the potential of the project to queer the classroom. She said of the approaches she observed in project schools and the discussions she had had with many team members:

> I felt that it is okay to be gay as long as you act kind of straight. Or like it's okay to have two mums or two dads as long as they are exactly the same as other families. You just kind of emphasise the whole sameness all the time which makes perfect sense of course, saying ah, it's the same love, everything is ... But you just get this really cute, nice, lovely and fluffy image that families are just great and fantastic and they are all the same really. And everything is adorable.

Introducing LGBT role models and fighting for LGBT acceptance can be seen as simply another form of tolerance discourse (Talburt and Steinberg, 2000). Yet Rasmussen (2006) points out that the introduction of non-heteronormative identity representations into pedagogic spaces through the normalisation of non-heterosexual family patterns threatens heteronormativity. She argues that to recognise similarities and normalities within the everyday is to undermine the subtle balance through which the absent Other marks and maintains the heteronormative centre: 'the avowal of different but equal ... is much less threatening than the avowal of similar and equal' (*ibid*:481). We found ourselves equally affected by these two different perspectives as the project developed and discussions between team members became deeper.

From role models to new commensurabilities

Youdell has written of the existence of 'impossible bodies,' certain identity constellations that are constituted in school as incommensurable (2006a). Elsewhere she has specifically analysed the incommensurability of gay with certain notions of masculinity, and the complex interplay between reinscription and recuperation enacted in a school setting (Youdell, 2004a). Recalling Andy's steadfast insistence on offering himself as a gay role model for his pupils, we consider here how this ostensibly essentialistic practice might involve a complex process of creating new commensurabilities. Deliberately introducing his unintelligible body into school, Andy struggles to remain comprehensible to his pupils as an out gay teacher:

Vignette 1: *Yes, I am a gay teacher!* (excerpt from Andy's field notes)
Andy: Advanced skills teacher
Sam: Year 5 pupil
Celia: Andy's teaching assistant (TA)

> It's Lunch time group in the Nurture Room. My TA Celia and I are having lunch with a group of six children from Year groups 3-6 who are considered to have 'challenging behaviour'. Sam has known me for five years, and, like all children in the school, knows that I have a male partner, and that I had a Civil Partnership ceremony.
>
> Sam walks to get a fork. As he returns he flops his wrist and says in a camp manner *I'm the only gay in the village*[3] (repeats this twice more) and sits down, grinning. The child next to him looks embarrassed and keeps looking at me for reassurance. I softly say Sam's name in a friendly but disappointed manner, expressing my disapproval: *Sam*.
>
> Sam repeats again: *I'm the only gay in the village*.
> looking directly at me. There is a slight air of confrontation about his doing this although it's more a humorous air. I think he expects me to laugh with him.
>
> Celia (TA): *Sam, can you stop that please*
>
> Sam: *Why?*
>
> Celia: *I don't like it*
>
> Sam: *Why?*

Andy: *Come on, Sam, you know why. Because I'm gay. It feels like you're making fun of me*

Sam: *You're not gay!*

Andy: *Sam, we've been through this. You know I'm gay.*

In this vignette we see the interplay between reinscription of a new kind of gay body (the authority figure, the well-known and respected teacher) and the recuperation of a gay body that is intelligible to Sam (a kind of comic self-deprecating gayness available to Sam via popular media in the figure of 'the only gay in the village'). Sam's understanding of 'gay' is constantly at risk of being subverted, but also constantly tending to recuperate, restabilise. This vignette illustrates both the powerful transformative potential of Andy's own gay body to unsettle Sam's certainties and the strong conservative potential of sedimented meanings (what 'gay' already means to Sam) to render Andy's gay body impossible to Sam.

Vignette 2: *Playing Monopoly with Andy's boyfriend* (excerpt from Andy's fieldnotes)
Andy: Advanced skills teacher
David: Andy's partner
Sam: Year 5 pupil
Celia: Andy's TA

On the last day of last half term I was being picked up from school by my partner after lunch. He arrived at school early and texted me from the car park so I texted back to say come in! So for the last fifteen minutes of lunch David joined me in my class with my lunchtime group. The interesting thing was that it just so happened that because of various events and absences I only had one child in with me, the child being the very same who had previously said 'you're not gay' and mimicked the 'Little Britain' character.

I said to him and my TA, Celia, *Oh David's here early, he's coming in to join us*, and the child visibly went white.

Sam: *David? Your... your... your...*
He didn't know what to say so I helped him out.

Andy: *My boyfriend, yes.*

Sam: *Coming? in here? now?*

Andy: *Yes – oh here he is!*

Honestly, the look on the poor child's face was a mixture of fascination and terror as David walked in and sat down next to me. I have never seen the child so quiet!

David joined the game of Monopoly with me and my TA and Sam for the next fifteen minutes, during which time Sam relaxed and had bits of conversation. There was a nice moment when the child's teacher, who knew David, came in and sat down with us and made conversation for a while. I couldn't have set it up better; this modelling of total acceptance!

Since returning to school after the holidays Sam has mentioned that he played Monopoly with David to the other children in both lunchtime sessions. He boasts about the fact that he has met Andy's boyfriend and *he* has played Monopoly with him! It will be interesting to see if over the next few months we have a repeat of the behaviour I saw from him previously.

This vignette reveals the transformative power of such a simple act as playing Monopoly with someone, once some of your basic assumptions about who those people can be and how they can be related to each other and to you have been destablised. Sam's initial discomfort (as evidenced by his obvious difficulty in voicing the simple phrase 'your boyfriend' to Andy) and eventual comfort (as evidenced by later declaring publicly that he has played Monopoly with this boyfriend) in this vignette is particularly interesting. It suggests that the very discomfort inspired by one's understandings being unsettled and destablised may be the key to what Butler describes as the productive practice of degrounding:

> Some people would say that we need a ground from which to act. We need a shared collective ground for collective action. I think we need to pursue the moments of degrounding, when we're standing in two different places at once; or we don't know exactly where we're standing; or when we've produced an aesthetic practice that shakes the ground. That's where resistance to recuperation happens. It's like a breaking through to a new set of paradigms. (Butler, Osborne and Segal, 1994:5)

Our research suggests that recuperation by dominant discourses comes all too easily, while reinscription requires not only momentary subversion, but persistence. It may not be enough to provide a momentary glimpse of new imaginaries (Atkinson and DePalma, 2008b); our research suggests that teachers must be constantly searching for these moments of degrounding, fleeting as they may be, and seize the opportunity not only to break down incommensurabilities but to make new possibilities. We do not intend to imply that this is a simple, progressive development; in fact, Andy's final reflection on Sam's possible future behaviour suggests that he is far from convinced that this work is finished.

Queering as impertinent visibility

Deborah Britzman (1995) identifies the methods of queer theory as 'impertinent' methods which subvert the norms of public discourse and go beyond the safe spaces of inclusion and equalities. She describes these methods as requiring an 'impertinent performance' and states:

> Some consider it [the term queer theory] as too angry, too oppositional – for what they imagine as the general public ... In fact, queer theory is an attempt to move away from psychological explanations like homophobia, which individualises heterosexual fear and loathing toward gay and lesbian subjects at the expense of examining how heterosexuality becomes normalised as natural. The subject of Queer Theory is more impertinent and more labile. (*ibid*:153)

Impertinence is, perhaps, one way of characterising moves made by project participants which are deliberately visible where they would normally be invisible. Deb writes in a web discussion:

> I snog in the street and experience it as a political act in the context of the tiny cathedral cities that I spend most of my time in ... I'm reminded that my everyday practice has effects, and that I can be tactical about that. I try not to get down about the all too ready recuperations...

McInnes suggests that a queer pedagogy, or rather what he describes as a 'pedagogy of incoherence' (2008:115) would enable us to 'pause at the moment of recognition,' taking 'a conceptual step back from ... the question of educational intervention' to 'work against the 'danger' within circuits of recognition whereby axes of recognition become solidified' (*ibid*:100). As a project team, we seem to be working in the spaces between recognition and solidification. Many of our *No Outsiders* classroom activities start, at least, with the impertinent visibility of that which has been categorically erased from children's (and many adults') realities. The question lies, in a sense, in where to go next.

14

Discovering that the heteronormal is not the only game in town may simply lead to broadening the norm to let in a few qualified fringe dwellers: trans men who fully transition and can 'pass', gay couples who mate for life and raise young together (like gay penguins do!). Even the best intentioned inclusion efforts render new exclusions, renegotiating borders rather than questioning how and why we build them. Would the new improved (non-hetero) normal have a place for people who are not interested in monogamy and child-rearing? What would happen if Andy had several casual boyfriends, rather than one life partner? What would happen if, instead of a young handsome trans man who was assigned 'girl' at birth, children met an older trans woman whom they initially read as a man in a dress? What would happen if they met a young person who resisted gender categories altogether, and whose sex/gender history was not easily traceable? Is there a way to dance quickly enough away from recognition to avoid being solidified, and is there a way to start from a less secure, less normalised, and less readable place?

There are many questions to be asked, and perhaps a great deal of certainty to unlearn, processes that are not particularly supported in school contexts where questions are usually raised only to be resolved as efficiently as possible. We are expected to keep things clear and simple for children, to worry about what they don't know when in fact we as a project team are more worried about what they already do know. Most people, school teachers and children included, are altogether too sure about what gender is: there are two 'opposite' sexes, man and woman, and gender is the inevitable categorical expression of natural sex. We learn to spot a gay person early on, even without any evidence about their sexual behaviour, and we are pretty sure what that means in terms of their behavior, preferences and relationships.

We even know which Teletubby is gay, and the tendency to 'out' celebrities, even fictional ones, only serves to reinforce our sense of expertise about gender and sexuality. Actress Jamie Lee Curtis must have been born intersex, goes the logic, because this explains everything, from her chiseled good looks, to her adopted children, to her gender-ambiguous name (see, for example, http://www.snopes.com/movies/actors/jamie.asp). Beloved comic book character Tin Tin was recently outed by gay journalist Matthew Parris, whose tongue-in-cheek exposé spares no details of the young man's (fictional) life:

> What debate can there be when the evidence is so overwhelmingly one-way? A callow, androgynous blonde-quiffed youth in funny trousers and a scarf moving into the country mansion of his best friend, a middle-aged sailor? A sweet-faced lad devoted to a fluffy white toy terrier ... whose only serious female friend is an opera diva ... And you're telling me Tintin isn't gay? (Parris, 2009)

Whether unsubstantiated Hollywood rumour or humorous journalistic rhetoric, our recognition of the inherent logic of these arguments reminds us of the extensive knowledge we share about gender and sexuality and how they are related. This is knowledge we have gained without teaching, knowledge that must be undone rather than replaced with newer, better knowledge. It doesn't matter (to us) what sort of genitals Jamie Lee Curtis was born with or whether Belgian cartoonist Georges Remi (Hergé) had a secret gay activist agenda over 100 years ago. Whether or not some of us start from a place of recognition, as *No Outsiders* project leaders we have been deeply interested in how to turn that recognition inside out: to unbelieve it, to unlearn it, to make of the familiar something strange and slippery and unsettling. The extent to which we have achieved this will remain open to debate – and is the subject of much discussion in the rest of this book. But the process of trying has, without a doubt, been enlightening for all of us.

Notes

1   We are including genderism, sexism and cissexism under the broader umbrella of heteronormativity, but these processes might well be examined as separate from or primary to heterosexism and heteronormativity; see, for example, (Airton, 2009; Serano, 2007).

2   This is a popular catchphrase of the only gay character in the comedy series *Little Britain*, aimed at an adult audience but widely watched by children.

2

Seeking a queer(ying) pedagogic praxis: Adventures in the classroom and participatory action research

Fin Cullen

In this chapter, Cullen focuses on the tensions between the methodological framing of the *No Outsiders* project as participatory action research and its interpretive/philosophical framing as a queer/feminist post-structuralist interrogation of hetero- and gender normativity. She explores ways in which these tensions might work both productively and as a closing force within the project, and brings considerations from both critical pedagogy and queer theory to bear on the possibility of a queer praxis which reshapes the classroom without simply either resisting or reproducing existing norms, examining specific examples of project interventions.

For much of my involvement with the *No Outsiders* project I struggled to comprehend the complexities of bridging theory, practice and policy to 'promote sexualities equality in the primary school'. Over the months, the team wrestled with what and how dissensus might be formed in the project, what a queer pedagogy might look like, ideas about social activism, political engagement, and pedagogy, and what might be realisable in the contemporary English primary classroom. This chapter emerges from these discussions, email exchanges and web postings, and the multiple voices and approaches drawn on at different points by members of the *No Outsiders* team.

The chapter explores the ways in which personal, professional and political identifications and theoretical approaches influenced by queer theory informed the school-based work. It critically reflects on how notions of praxis might help to examine how theory and practice were used by teacher researchers. The *No Outsiders* project as participatory action research has valued the joint production and creation of knowledge in creating critically reflective approaches to challenging homophobia and promoting gender and sexualities equality.

Through an examination of some of the pedagogic strategies deployed in the *No Outsiders* project, I want to highlight how earlier ideas of activism, civic engagement and lesbian and gay rights continued to mark this project for the participants. Accordingly I explore lines of convergence between such approaches and the politics and theoretical potential offered by queer theory within the space of the school. By doing so, I want to examine the potential of a queer praxis, and the challenges and opportunities in imagining critical classroom pedagogies that might unpack hierarchical sex/gender discourses in play within schools.

This is not always easy, as has been noted by scholars writing about queer pedagogy over the past decade or so (Britzman, 1995; Sears, 1999; Blaise, 2005). As O'Rourke (2007) acknowledges, there are dangers in collapsing and collating queer theory and lesbian and gay studies. For example, in recent years there has been increasing acknowledgement of the differences between queer and LGBT approaches and of the potential risk of completely losing sight of queer theory's questioning of normalcy in lesbian and gay studies' exploration of lesbian and gay histories and representation, calls for LGB equalities and challenges to heterosexism and homophobia.

Much of the influential theoretical work that provided an immensely helpful conceptual framework was that of Butler (1993) in de-essentialising naturalised categories and critiquing sex/gender binaries and conceptual binaries of bodily sex, gender and sexuality that had marked earlier writings in feminist and gay and lesbian studies. The concept of heteronormativity also proved useful in examining how the positioning of binary sex/gender privileges and legitimises heterosexual desire and gender above all other gendered and sexualised identities (Ingraham, 1994; Letts, 1999). Work by education scholars has further explored how such conceptual tools can aid researchers' understandings of how the repetition of signifying discourses upholds and reproduces enduring sex/gender binaries and normative heterosexuality within early years and school settings (Britzman, 1995; Francis, 1998; Epstein, 1999; Sears, 1999; Renold, 2005; Blaise, 2005; DePalma and Atkinson; 2007a).

No Outsiders as a project attempts to link practical work influenced by diversity management perspectives and LGBT identity work with theoretical work drawing on critical pedagogies and queer and feminist post-structuralist theory. Lesbian and gay-identified teacher researchers often took a more personal, organic approach by being 'out' in the school community, an attempt to provide a positive gay role model for their students (see Chapter 5). Other approaches were resource-led, including literacy, drama and arts work, such as co-writing with pupils a libretto based on one of the project books or using the picture books during assemblies, literacy sessions and circle time. Another resources-based approach, which I discuss later, was illustrated by one teacher who chose to 'gender trouble' the gender identity of everyday maths worksheets as a way of engaging primary children in debates about sex/gender discourses. The wide variety of approaches taken by participants in this project allows us to consider how a wide selection of approaches, strategies and modes of analysis may contribute to providing a more nuanced understanding of what a queer(ying) pedagogy might resemble.

Locating praxis

How might the project be engaged in 'shaping the world' (M Smith, 1994:162)? As a participatory action research project, *No Outsiders* owes a debt to earlier emancipatory projects by radical educators influenced by Freirian pedagogy (Freire, 1972) with a commitment to dialogue and consciousness-raising among disenfranchised groups. The multiple uses of notions of praxis within critical and feminist pedagogy and action research has been explored by Weiner (1994), who argues for the continued use of a feminist praxis in interrogating gender inequality within school. Notions of praxis also influence the development of some action research approaches (*ibid*). The *action* of action research within schools and education settings is about shaping pedagogy and developing curriculum resources, which involves peer learning and bridging the gap between academic theory and practice. As the *No Outsiders*' website states:

> The *No Outsiders* research project was designed according to the participatory action research (PAR) model, which links practice and systematic reflection to form a powerful type of research that draws upon practitioner strengths in ways that traditional academic research has failed to recognise:
>
>> 'It is now widely recognised that practitioners have unique insights into practice which are simply not available to researchers who come in from outside, and that professional knowledge is, therefore, an essential component of understanding any educational practice.' (Somekh, 2005, p 3) (available at http://www.nooutsiders.sunderland.ac.uk/about-the-project)

Action research models that arose from the 1970s started with knowledgeable practitioners who critically reflected on their practice and engaged in dialogue with students in exploring the nature of social justice. Such an approach generated spaces for critical reflection and action intended to create interventions that might shape practice. These models take as given the need for ground-up solutions to the problems of social inequalities as well as subjects that are fixed in their raced, gendered and sexual identities and thus can mobilise around such issues. Kincheloe (1991) argues that teacher research as a democratic form can work as a catalyst for political action and social change. Kincheloe's view might be seen as idealistic, as the appropriation of some teacher research within 'good practice' models may be about upholding narrow neo-liberal models of education rather than mounting robust critiques. However, research that is reflective and critically engaged might begin to unpack some of the discursive formations of the dominant social order.

I am also keen to tease out the selection of approaches that might be contained in the project subtitle 'researching sexualities equality.' The *No Outsiders* project has been influenced on a substantive, epistemological and methodological level by feminist post-structuralist and queer theoretical analysis. In an array of seminar papers, articles and films, it has also been shaped methodologically by the postmodern turn within ethnography (Clifford, 1986). For example, the chapter in this collection by Atkinson and Moffat is constructed so as to emphasise dialogue between the multiple voices of the project team and is re-

miniscent of postmodern influenced approaches to composing ethnography (Ellis and Bochner, 1996).

The layers of interpretation and what might constitute data in such a
collaborative effort complicates the notion of a single line of enquiry
with a set and finite conclusion. Such diversity in approach may complicate the claims that might be made for the emerging data. The notion
of 'dissensus' has been drawn on throughout the project to acknowledge this diversity of voice. However, whilst notions of praxis may sit
comfortably with dialogue and dissensus, such an often fluid account
may not easily translate into clear pedagogic tools for the primary classroom. The gay and lesbian equalities work has a much clearer outcome
base in both challenging homophobia and heterosexism via discrete
curriculum and policy interventions such as homophobic bullying
policies, support groups for gay teachers and parents, the use of books
with non-heterosexual characters, diverse families and storylines and
the inclusion of same sex relationships in Sex and Relationships education.

So what's queer about queer pedagogy?

Heteronormativity is replicated and sustained through the early years
and primary school via formal and hidden curricula, the perceived
centrality of the nuclear heterosexual family unit, the invisibility in
classroom texts and in many schools of 'out' lesbian, gay, bisexual, trans
(LGBT) or queer people and the lack of acknowledgment of LGBT or
queer parents (Thorne, 1993; Davies, 1993; Epstein, 1997; Epstein, 1999;
Renold, 2005; Atkinson and DePalma, 2008b). If O'Rourke (2007) is correct that queer theory within the academy has recently been increasingly institutionalised and domesticated in its potential conflation with
lesbian and gay studies, it is worth revisiting what might be imagined to
constitute a queer pedagogy within schools. This would go beyond
pedagogic approaches that examined lesbian and gay rights or issues of
sex and sexuality. Britzman states that a queer pedagogy would attempt
to:

> ... exceed such binary oppositions as the tolerant and the tolerated and the
> oppressed and the oppressor yet still hold onto an analysis of social dif-
> ference that can account for how structural dynamics of subordination and
> subjection work at the level of the historical, the conceptual, the social, and

21

the psychic. ... These identifications I take as the beginnings of a queer peda-gogy, one that refuses normal practices and practices of normalcy, one that begins with an ethical concern for one's own reading practices, one that is interested in exploring what one cannot bear to know, one interested in the imagining of a sociality unhinged from the dominant conceptual order. (1995: 164-165)

Following Britzman and work by Blaise (2005) I examine some of these tensions between a modernist project of participatory action research intended to shape pedagogic interventions and the wider discourse of troubling normalcy offered by Britzman's critique. In relation to participatory action research and the *No Outsiders* research project, there remain issues in thinking about whether school-based interven-tions could question and challenge normalcy in the ways in which Britzman suggests or even fundamentally begin to challenge binary sex/gender and/or sexuality. Not that it is easy to separate sex-gender from sexuality: the presumed normalcy and fixity enshrined in lan-guage of a binary sex/gender system (girl/boy; gay/straight) remains predicated upon notions of heterosexuality (Butler, 1993). I return later to the difficulties in moving beyond such binaries.

At first glance, the connections between feminist post-structuralism and queer theories and the school classroom may not be immediately apparent. The theoretical thrust of queer theory and 'gender trouble' (Butler, 1990) within this project was treated with perhaps some under-standable scepticism by many of the school-based teacher researchers, who saw it as over-theoretical, the preserve of academia, and not easily or straightforwardly translatable into classroom practice. This difficulty in translating such an analytical frame to school practice has been noted by Pascoe (2007) who, in an ethnography of the 'anti-fag dis-course' in a US high school, noted that translating feminist post-struc-turalist work to classroom interventions may not always be straight-forward.

A queer praxis within education as a post-identity project may not be synonymous with gay and lesbian identities (LG with the silent B and T), and potentially may be seen to render suspect such fixed sexual identities. To follow Britzman (1995) and think the unthinkable or con-sider 'queerying pedagogy [as] queerying its technics and scribbling graffiti over its texts, of colouring outside the lines' (Bryson and de

Castell, 1993:299), would go well beyond institutionally and state sanctioned 'diversity management' (Mohanty, 1990: 299).

No Outsiders team member Deborah Youdell has argued for a range of tactics for a performative political pedagogy (2007). These included a troubling of normative constitutions of schooling and of subject positions, and the need to offer students opportunities to deconstruct these positions and re-deploy the discourses that locate them (see Chapter 3). Such approaches might prove challenging within the frameworks of the *No Outsiders* project as realised within contemporary English classrooms, particularly if teachers do not wish to be read as unduly radical or wish the project to be in accord with and legible within current policy initiatives around, for example, inclusion. Like Youdell, I am not attempting to evaluate these interventions set against a backdrop of being sufficiently queer. However, I would argue that there have occasionally been instances where teachers have used picture books, drama work or other interventions to begin to trouble the regulatory normative discourses underpinning the sex/gender identities in play. Designing and delivering critical pedagogic interventions based on feminist post-structuralist or queer theoretical thoughts may differ substantially from engagements which lend themselves to queer analysis in accidental or playful inversion and troubling of heteronormativity.

Such theoretical underpinnings potentially have uses as a method or tool of analysis. Queer theories tended to be used in the project as an analytical tool in exploring data from the field rather than as an ongoing legible pedagogic intervention in the classroom. However, work which is largely framed within such diversity management discourses might mobilise everyday resistances rather than deeply trouble the normative constitutions of schooling. Britzman's notion of queer pedagogy might help us consider alternatives.

On one level approaches influenced by critical pedagogy might be considered incommensurable with the slipperiness of tangled, fragmented and discursive sex/gender identities. Furthermore, as scholars have noted, it is in the intersections between class, race, gender, (dis)ability, generation and sexual identities that performances shape discursive selves (Youdell, 2006; Mirza, 2008). Any approach that teases out just one of these identity constellations (Youdell, 2006) in isolation is going to be potentially problematic. The traditions of gay (and lesbian) rights-based educational work might form an easier fit when drawing on a relatively linear action research model to seek given legible solutions to the problems of homophobia and heterosexism.

Yet the *No Outsiders* research team have at different points drawn on divergent critical approaches including aspects of liberal humanism, critical pedagogy, queer theory and feminist post-structuralism. The project as realised within pedagogic intervention within classrooms was predominantly based on this rights-based model of practice and several of the research team were involved in debating what a queer(ying) pedagogy might resemble. Our discussions on the features of a queer pedagogy, such as the engagement with deconstruction, dialogue and unpacking of taken-for-granted categories reminded me of earlier notions of critical and feminist pedagogy. One practitioner spoke about how her use of forum theatre techniques and a non-heterosexual fairytale character was directly influenced by critical pedagogic approaches such as Freire (1972), in addition to queer and feminist post-structuralist writings, notably Butler's work on unfixing sex/gender binaries.

This is not to say a queer praxis involving queer pedagogues and pedagogy cannot exist in the current education climate in the UK. Nor do I want to fall into the trap of the binary. This work is not about:

LGBT equalities vs. queer
Practice vs. theory
School vs. Academy

These either/or classifications are misnomers. But merely heading all these subtleties under a broad notion of dissensus does a disservice to the intricate hierarchies of power, knowledge and practice that might be in play. The complexities and potential incongruity in such approaches are reflected in Spivak's conditional call for a 'strategic essentialism' (1988), and in Butler's implicit acknowledgement of the need for occasional strategic use of 'universality' in subsequent LGBT rights work (Butler, 1999a:viii).

The potential within feminist post-structuralism and queer theories for rejecting grand narratives and acknowledging shifting, multiple, complex and reflexive subjectivities might thus be enabling rather than challenging theories of gender, power, praxis and pedagogy. Coffey and

Delamont (2000) argue that this engagement with postmodern theories enables scholars to formulate new critiques by illustrating the nuanced complexities and contexts of how such power and inequality are operationalised within educational contexts. For Paechter (2001), the focus on the centrality of the text and materiality of the body in post-structuralist thought provides potential for scholars to interrogate power relations, the production and interrogation of curriculum texts and the production of gender performances. The *No Outsiders* project has taken a similar starting point, focusing on experience rather than a given set of methods or approaches.

Whether one commences inquiry based on a premise of LGBT equalities and a recognition of the centrality of the sex/gender binary or instead wishes to challenge fixed boundaries and trouble notions of normalcy within the field settings fundamentally shapes both the research method and legible interventions that spring from this epistemological base. Of course, legibility may not be a desirable or anticipated outcome for queer pedagogues who wish to unpick and question normalcy.

Such queer pedagogies are replicated throughout multiple instantiations of the *No Outsiders* project as the resources were utilised in schools and arts and drama projects were developed. The research team's reflections, interviews and resources illustrate that teachers were engaged in ongoing discussions with pupils in thinking through and being critical of normative gendered and sexualised discourses. Such approaches can complicate, even temporarily, the everyday sex/gendered subjectivities within the primary classroom but have rarely reached the deeper interrogations identified by scholars (Britzman, 1995; Blaise, 2005; Youdell, 2007) in fundamentally examining the normalcy of school relations and the primacy of the educator's agenda. The next section acknowledges the project's debt to professional and activist selves in enabling individuals to engage with debates around gender and sexualities equality in school.

Past selves and present teaching

How, then, did practitioners use their own autobiographies, identities, and political engagement to shape their work and how did this impact on their adoption, reappropriation or rejection of theorisations originating in post structuralism and queer theories? Several teachers had

25

experience of activism within social movements such as student politics, faith groups, environmental activism, lesbian and gay rights groups and trade union work and this framed their attraction to and participation in the *No Outsiders* project:

> I was worried at the beginning that the project might have been to do with flag waving or had a political agenda. I didn't want that, but now I'm finding myself wanting to lobby MPs and whatever it takes. I suppose because of the 'rightness' of what I'm discovering. .. I did have internal doubts, but haven't for a few years now. I have always tried to stand up against injustice and, as a student, did the CND [UK-based anti-nuclear campaign] marches and the boycotting of Barclays etc. Some of that earlier fervour seems to be re-emerging. (Sue, web posting)

For Sue, a head teacher, the rightness of challenging social injustice validates her involvement in the project, as she narrates it as part of a wider history of movements for social justice.

The ghost of section 28[4] haunted this project, even though it was repealed in England in 2003 and in Scotland in 2000. The damaging and limiting effects of this pernicious piece of legislation had affected many of the teachers earlier in their careers and continued to affect their personal and professional identities at school. One teacher researcher spoke about how the project could engender a sense of optimism in the wake of the distress of the Section 28 attack:

> Jo: When Clause 28 was introduced I was in my early twenties. It was quite a distressing time, it felt that society was going in a very negative direction ... Now it feels things are changing ...
>
> Elizabeth: Has it [your involvement in the project, or in anti-homophobic work generally] re-radicalised you in any way ...?
>
> Jo: In doing that [doing anti-homophobic work in school] ... it means probably I've come up against negative attitudes and have had to challenge them ... For so long I've only talked to people who are like-minded.
>
> (Jo – in interview with Elizabeth Atkinson)

Other teacher researchers spoke candidly about how their involvement in the project had reawakened their previous activist selves. For teachers who identified as lesbian or gay, coming out to parents, colleagues or pupils was seen as a deeply personal and politically engaged

act, reminiscent of the political and personal transformation characteristic of earlier participatory research studies within education
(Griffin, 1992). However, not all gay and lesbian identified teacher researchers felt they could be 'out' to colleagues in school. In some
schools, teachers were unsupported by school leadership in coming out
to pupils because this was seen as a purely personal matter rather than
one of political and wider significance (for discussion on the some of
the tensions for research participants in discussing sexualities equality
in primary school see DePalma and Atkinson, 2009).

This understanding of teaching and involvement in the *No Outsiders*
project as a political act engaged in an everyday form of social action
was clearly articulated by many of the participants. This is not to say
that this work was a bolt-on political project, rather that the *No Outsiders* project and a commitment to sexualities equality and a wider
inclusion agenda informed teachers' everyday practice and shaped the
development of education interventions and schemes of work. The *No
Outsider* project also gave an explicit permission to discuss relevant
issues in challenging homophobia and promoting sexualities equality
with colleagues including support staff such as lunchtime supervisors.

Several teacher researchers brought into their practice their academic
study at universities before they commenced their teaching career,
which had provided an engagement with critical theory. One parti-
cipant's university study of sociology, feminist activism and familiarity
with key academic figures shaped her commitment to equalities work
in her career:

> I remember being at university and the only thing that I wanted to be was an
> equalities officer ... I was at university in the late seventies and the sociology
> agenda had just been discovered ... Ken Plummer was professor there ... and
> he was hugely influential in my development. (Annie, taped discussion with
> Fin)

Annie's commitment to gender equality translated into a commitment
to support a scheme of emotional literacy work within schools in her
local authority. Whether teachers had been involved in peace or
women's movements, anti-Section 28 protests or trade unionism, such
histories informed the values, practice base and identities of the researchers with a commitment to social justice. This grounding of the

project's participants in earlier activism led at times to an understandable wariness of the fluidity around post-structuralism and queer theory and politics, as such activist groups had drawn upon clearly defined identity positions to make political rights-based claims.

Theory-implicit and explicit approaches

The *No Outsiders* team consisted of practitioners based in universities, schools, early years settings and local authorities. Such a breadth of involvement inevitably involved a diversity of personal political histories, opinions, approaches and engagement with practice and theory. Andy, a teacher researcher, articulated a reluctance and wariness about ideas of the academy and theory in general that was echoed by other teacher researchers:

> I am absolutely not big on theory, but I just choose not to go into those sorts of things. I have been in on the web, I tend to write very sort of practical things and then someone [else], they will come up and [write something] really big into theory. And I am thinking oh God, I don't know what to say now so I will write something about I did this today and I ignored all the theory stuff completely ... It's not that I say that I am not taking it in, it's just not something that I am particularly hot on really. (Andy, taped discussion with Fin)

Not being hot on theory was not necessarily a rejection of theoretical underpinnings or the work of the academy. Rather, there was a sense that theory was remote and steeped in inaccessible language that was not easily translatable to the everyday of the school classroom (see Chapter 8). Such tensions are particularly acute when dealing with feminist post-structuralism and queer theories; aspects of Butler's works on the need to challenge the enduring nature of the heterosexual matrix (1993) and heteronormativity (Ingraham, 1994) might appear alien and incomprehensible to those unfamiliar with academic debates and language. The academy, as represented by academic writings and the theoretical concerns of the university-based researchers, could appear both abstract and remote from the everyday concerns of practice. Arguably, the certainties of fixed gender and sexual identities as legible political subjects are more intelligible in relation to the policy discourse available to a school or local authority than the abstract notions behind 'gender trouble'. To 'queer' could be viewed with disdain, particularly with echoes of an earlier painful, pejorative voice experienced by some of the teacher researchers as an interpellation of hate. The word 'queer' has a particular charge when talking about education (Sears, 1999).

Queer theory, with a focus on unpacking normalcy, challenges the foundations of lesbian and gay studies in examining and destabilising fixed lesbian and gay identities (Sorkin Rabinowitz, 2002). Such contradictions and tensions were observable within this project. As one teacher researcher highlights below, the political endeavour of his project work required him to concentrate on lesbian and gay identities:

> Fin: Do the children ever quiz you or query you about that someone might love a man and a woman?
>
> Andy: No. I haven't had that yet. No, no.
>
> Fin: How would you handle it?
>
> Andy: I haven't handled it yet. I have gone down the line that you are gay or you are straight. That's the line that I've gone down. Because I want to make the argument to almost try and adjust that homophobic attitude that you choose to be gay. I am saying you don't choose to be gay, you are or you are not. It simplifies it, doesn't it? (Andy, taped discussion with Fin)

The 'fixed' essential binary sexual subject was perceived by several members of the research team as simpler and much easier to talk about to children, parents and colleagues than the confusing fluidity of 'queer.' For Andy, being gay needs to remain a fixed identity in order to avoid collapsing into the politically dangerous rhetoric of choice. Andy's approach to sexualities equality is primarily about consolidation and opening up dialogue about lesbian and gay identities rather than problematising the normalcy of heterosexuality. Andy is being strategic in his deployment and use of essential binary categories. It is not that he cannot grasp queer theory but that he sees it as potentially undermining his wider political agenda in supporting valuable sexualities equality work within his setting.

Such a position privileges the need to meet adults and children alike where they are at over the abstract language of the academy and is seen as a first step in a much larger politically engaged educational project supporting social justice. The need to simplify sexual categories into gay or straight and to acknowledge that gay people exist is seen as the fundamental work of the project and this work is particularly facilitated by the use of the project's storybooks. This endeavour is not about interrogating heterosexuality but about finding space for gay and lesbian identities to be acknowledged and perhaps celebrated within schools and the community. Such a focus on inclusion and diversity formed a strong central theme in much of the project's classroom-based work.

However, whilst several teacher researchers took a pragmatic route and chose not to engage directly with the slipperiness of queer theory, other teacher researchers explicitly used such theory to complicate and trouble sex/gender binaries by entering into dialogue with pupils and other teaching staff. For example, Laura used interventions inspired by feminist post-structuralist thought to work with the children in writing alternative fairytales, designing maths worksheets that destabilise gender and using drama work to produce a non-traditional Cinderella character who spoke about her fictional girlfriend (Cullen and Sandy, 2009). Such approaches included entering into dialogue about gendered discourses with children, unpicking the norms of heterosexual gender, and 'gender troubling' everyday classroom items, such as the aforementioned maths worksheet. As Laura explained:

> I drew a person that looked, I would say unmistakably if we're talking in terms of what is conventional, like a girl. But I called the person James. The kids could not get their heads around it. [One child] asked if he could cross the name out and change it to a girl's name. I asked why he wanted to do that. 'Because it's not a boy!' he replied. 'How do you know?' I asked. 'Because he is wearing a bow in his hair.' 'But can't boys wear bows in their hair?' I asked. At this point the group of six children all laughed and told me no, boys can't wear bows in their hair. Of course I asked 'Why not?' [The child who wanted to change the name] told me 'boys wear bows around their necks not on their heads'. I commented that I had never heard of anything like that and that I thought anyone could wear a bow wherever they liked! (Laura, web posting)

This example of a gender-troubling maths worksheet is not meant to represent a 'valid' example of an appropriate intervention. I am reminded in various interventions of how the queerying of sex/gender regulatory framings might take place alongside a partial recuperation of the heterosexual matrix. The slipperiness of this work might suggest that even in diversity discourses we might both uphold and negate such regulatory framings. The fixed unitary subject positions of the boys' and girls' naming and attire are recognised and questioned by the pupils in the classroom discussions, but the essential nature of the fixed gender binary arguably remains. Laura subverts the binary, but does not dismantle it entirely. The brief troubling of the gendered signifiers remains temporal and contextual and does not trickle out beyond this brief queer(ying) moment into the wider curriculum or classroom resources.

However, Laura is trying here to answer directly the calls by scholars seeking a queer pedagogy (Bryson and de Castell, 1993; Britzman, 1995; Blaise, 1995; Sears, 1999) by engaging children in a dialogue to interrogate the implicit sexual binary underpinning gender norms. Laura's adventures in creating maths worksheets to challenge fixed notions of gender might still revolve around the gender binaries, but they do start to unpick key signifiers: the bow, the long eyelashes. The issue with such an approach is that without returning to unpack this with the children or continuing to discuss gender-regulatory discourses, this work may seem remote and difficult to replicate and pass unnoticed in terms of regulatory framings around what might be legitimately recognised as 'good teaching.'

In fact, Laura's engagement with queer theory was not without challenge from other teaching staff within her school. Laura reminds us that while queer may be a legitimate frame for university researchers, it remains potential anathema in the primary school. When she spoke with a deputy head in her school about the educational potential in 'queer', she was greeted with bemusement:

> My deputy head said I had too much time on my hands if I was thinking about fluid identities and troubling boundaries! I tried to explain how it could impact on the way we teach identity but I think he didn't like the way I couldn't put my finger on exactly what it is to 'do queer.' And my attempts were rather lame. (Laura, web posting)

Laura is concerned that the term 'queer' might strike the school management as unduly radical, yet she remains committed to using queer theory in framing and thinking through classroom interventions. One of the personal challenges I have explored during the latter part of my involvement in this research project has been about teasing out some of the individual participants' perspectives on such theoretical approaches and exploring how they inform ideas about what might be do-able in the classroom. Laura's rebuke from her deputy head that she must have 'too much time on [her] hands' is an explicit critique of such theoretical work as not being engaged in the real activities of the class-room and school. Such a critique served to compromise Laura's ability to be an educational professional *and* queer theorist.

As this work progressed I became increasingly aware of how such micro-moments of interaction can start the process of thinking the un-thinkable (Britzman, 1995) within everyday classroom interaction, yet how such moments may be fleeting and are not as legible as a whole-school anti-bullying workshop or an assembly on gay historical figures. Such approaches have ties with the dialogic elements in earlier work regarding education and praxis. They produce critical reflection but there remains a need to take heed of the ways in which heteronorma-tivity and other regulatory hierarchical framings may be reinscribed and reframed, as Youdell argues in Chapter 3.

Tactics and strategies – some further thoughts

My involvement as a researcher in this project has been deeply chal-lenging and enlightening. It has provided insights into how post-struc-turalist theory can be difficult to translate into legible classroom prac-tice within the neoliberal school. It has led me to contemplate whether the essential categories of gender and sexual orientation are, at least some of the time, important tools for analysing and thinking through how such regulatory framings endure. As a diverse project, *No Outsiders* became a ground for interventions in terms of LGBT equalities in class-room lessons, diversity management training and policy support alongside a minority of theoretically motivated and inspired interven-tions by classroom teachers.

This is not to say that day-to-day practice within schools is not fertile ground for queer analysis. Recent ethnographies provide ample testi-mony to the enduring possibilities of a queer eye (Sears, 1999; Renold, 2005; Blaise, 2005; Youdell, 2007) in unpicking and querying how heteronormative discourses are sustained and recuperated. In the *No Outsiders* project, queer theory as an analytic tool similarly provided much scope for sketching out the productive and fruitful work that was developing within a largely LGBT rights-based epistemological framing. Bringing theory and action together in a search for queer praxis raises many questions about what is legible and perceived to be teachable within primary schools and what might be legitimately and strategically drawn on to develop this work further. This work constitutes learner and teacher identities in myriad ways and troubles normative notions of pedagogy within early years and primary settings.

Acknowledgements

I would like to extend my gratitude to everyone in the No Outsiders Research team. Special thanks are due to Deborah Youdell, Renée DePalma, Elizabeth Atkinson, Sandy Allan and especially Andy and Laura for insightful conversations and comments on earlier versions of this chapter.

Note

4   Section 28 of the Local Government Act 1988 stated that a local authority 'shall not intentionally promote homosexuality or publish material with the intention of promoting homosexuality' or 'promote the teaching in any maintained school of the acceptability of homosexuality as a pretended family relationship'.

3

Lessons in praxis: thinking about knowledge, subjectivity, and politics in education

Deborah Youdell

In this chapter, Youdell illustrates the (im)possibility of taking a queer stance in a world constituted by normative discourse, and explores the impact of these normative constructions on the project's work. She unpacks the normative forces which have shaped the project, while at the same time suggesting that some of its work can be read simultaneously as both critical (and potentially normative) social action and queer troubling. She suggests ways forward for work in this field which acknowledge philosophical differences in relation to knowledge and knowledge construction and work with rather than against such differences, while recognising their particular effects.

Introduction

This chapter considers what it means to engage in forms of politically inflected practice concerned with sexualities inside schools. These practices and the politics that underpin them might aim to challenge homophobia, enact anti-homophobic teaching, pursue sexualities equality, interrupt heteronormativity, enable multiple and mobile sex-gender-sexuality identifications and locations to be recognisable and legitimate or move beyond sexed-gendered-sexualised subjectivities. Embedded in each of these potential goals and the ways that they are expressed here is a set of conceptual tools and an approach to politics and change. These might be characterised as liberal reform politics, as identity politics or as queer politics. The relationship between conceptual tools, political modes and political goals is an important one, but it is also one that is subject to slippage and which can be difficult to track. In this chapter I try to map some of the connections between political philosophies, goals and practices available to and taken up by the *No Outsiders* project.

In particular, I explore the notion of 'queer' and its politics that have come out of wider post-structurally informed thinking about power and resistance. I set this alongside contemporary Left radical politics in education and borrow the notion of praxis, the joining together of theory and practice, to think tactically about the sorts of political practices we might engage in and the effects, wanted and unwanted, that these might have. I consider the possibilities for and implications of multiple political philosophies and associated tactics coexisting within a body of social and political action. I argue that politics in education is inevitably marked by undecidability concerning political philosophies, goals, practices and effects and that, discomforting as this undecidability may be, it is the condition of our work and may well be the condition of its possibility too.

Considering queer practices and politics

My thinking about 'queer' is located in Michel Foucault's (1990b) *History of Sexuality Volume 1: An introduction*, a location that makes queer inseparable, for me, from the work of Foucault and the more recent thinking that has come out of this. This conceptual framework makes queer about interrogating how discourses of sex and sexuality are implicated in the processes through which we are made as 'subjects' who are sexed and sexualised in particular ways. Judith Butler's *Imitation and Gender Insubordination* (1991) and Eve Sedgwick's *Epistemology of the Closet* (1993) are early pieces that powerfully demonstrated the illusion of the preceding, unitary, self-knowing and *sexed* and *sexualised* subject and the way that gay and lesbian identities and identity politics are implicated in the constitution of these subjects. Queer is also about resisting these processes through practices that unsettle the meanings of these discourses and deploy other discourses that have been subjugated, disallowed or silenced (Butler, 1997). The take-up of the name 'queer', with its history of injury, and the re-deployment of queer in order to make it mean something different and make sense in new ways and in places where it has only been injurious or where it has been wholly disallowed, is a key aspect of the politics of this thinking. In this way, queer has sometimes been deployed tactically as 'who we are'. But in the spirit of the theory that it draws upon, it has not been who we really are, because 'who we *really* are' is rejected by the queer theory that insists instead on practices – the bodies and pleasures, freed from regimes of sex and desire, of Foucault's imagination (1990a).

Judith Butler (1999b) has usefully engaged Foucault's imagined replacement of subjects made known and knowable though prevailing accounts of sex and desire with mobile and multiple bodies and pleasures that exceed these accounts. She argues that while Foucault's 'rallying cry' has been massively important politically, in practice the force of the dominant meanings of sex and desire is not as easily undercut as Foucault's call to bodies and pleasures might be seen to infer. We might assert bodies and pleasures and refuse the binaries of penis/vagina, man/woman, hetero/homo, and yet prevailing discourse presses these upon us, like it or not. We might struggle to refuse these subjectivities, but subject-hood is dependent on our intelligibility and so we might have to take them up; we might find them put on us; and we might be attached to them politically, socially, relationally, psychically.

In my previous research and writing concerned with sexualities and schooling I have taken up Butler's (1990; 1993; 1997; 2004) understanding of performativity and subjectivation in and through the heterosexual matrix to make sense of how a sexed and sexualised subject comes to be 'who' s/he is in school contexts. This framework rejects the rationality, permanence and coherence that characterise prevailing accounts of the subject. Instead it offers a conception of a subject who is subject to and made subject by relations of power in an ongoing way, and yet comes to appear abiding and self-knowing through these processes of subjectivation (Butler, 1997, 2004). My work in this area (Youdell, 2003, 2004a; 2004b; 2005; 2006a) is part of a body of poststructural work that has explored the circulation of discourses in education, the way these are implicated in constituting particular subjects of education and the ways in which these subjects resist or reinscribe these subjectivities (see Davies *et al*, 2001; Rassmussen and Harwood,

37

2003; Rasmussen *et al*, 2004; Renold, 2006). This work has also turned to queer, deconstructive and performative politics to think about how the practices, meanings and subjects inside schools and classrooms might be shifted (Atkinson and DePalma, 2009; Hey, 2006; Rasmussen, 2006; Talburt and Steinberg, 2000; Youdell, 2006a; 2006b). Such thinking has looked to trouble normative constitutions of schooled subjectivities and rupture the borders of intelligibility. It sets out to offer young people tools to deconstruct their social and educational location, tactically redeploy the discourses that locate them and resist the recuperation of their practices (Davies, 1993; Kopelson, 2002; Youdell, 2006a).

In this chapter I put these ideas to work in an effort to make sense of the politics and practices of the *No Outsiders* project and, most importantly, to think about the possible effects these practices might have. In the context of a project framed expressly by queer conceptual tools and which aims to take up and enact a queer politics, such a move needs to be taken with caution. My intention is not to identify examples of work from the project and consider their queer possibilities and/or failures. Rather it is to contribute to the thinking through of the effects, the misfires and the recuperations of our practices as part of the wider work of the project team in this collection and elsewhere (Atkinson and DePalma, 2009; Cullen and Sandy, 2009; DePalma and Atkinson, 2009; DePalma and Teague, this volume). Nevertheless, as I approached accounts of practice in project schools and classrooms, data generated through the project's web-discussions and my own participation in project events and meetings, I was discomforted by the imagined requirement that I place these under the gaze of my theoretical lens and weigh up what was queer and what was not. In a project team of 30 plus, these acts of weighing-up can neither be wholly collaborative nor be expected to lead to consensus. And while the space for, indeed the desire for, dissensus is written into the project design, in a setting framed by the tradition of collaboration and consensus, dissensus is harder to do than to say. Furthermore, solo readings of the practices of others with whom one is, in principle, collaborating are not the same as reading ethnography already abstracted from those about whose practices it speaks, and such readings magnify the ethical problems of authority and voice in research (Lather, 1991; Stanley and Wise, 1993; St Pierre and Pillow, 2000).

Rather than weighing up the specificities of particular project interventions (yes, dear, lovely queer classroom, have a gold star and a glass of champagne! Sorry dear, you really haven't got the hang of this queer thing have you? Do try to pay more attention in team development days, oh, and stop calling me homosexual would you?), this chapter considers the project's multiple conceptual framings and the implications of these for our practices and their effects. At the heart of my discomfort over any potential evaluative aspect to my consideration is the risk of imposing a set of theoretical and political ideas as a framework when those theoretical and political ideas would resist such singular and singularlising imposition. And alongside this is my recognition that in its praxis the work of the project is not simply or solely queer (or post-structural, or Foucauldian). So I do not identify 'exemplars' of 'queer' practice in the project's work, an identification which would inevitably assume and constitute my position of/as authority and indirectly criticise that work not singled out. Instead I explore the fractures between and intersections across the *multiple* ways in which knowledge, the subject, politics and sexuality are understood and enacted in the project and suggest some of the implications of this multiplicity. I argue that the practices of the project suggest simultaneously that:

- knowledge is constituted *and* that it is self-evident

- the subject is constituted through ongoing discursive practices *and* that, while diverse, subjects are unitary and enduring

- political practices take the form of discursive insurrections that unsettle prevailing knowledges, meanings and subject positions *and* that political practices correct erroneous knowledges and representations and assert the rights of diverse disenfranchised individuals.

Versions of knowledge: constitutions and truth

A Foucauldian account of discourse and disciplinary power identifies the constituted and productive nature of knowledge at the same time as it underscores the indivisibility of power and knowledge (Foucault, 1990b, 1991). Central to Foucault's understanding and his project is the inquiry into how a particular set of ideas comes to attain the status of truth in a given context and moment; he does not ask 'Is this true? or 'Is this more or less true that that?' but 'How does this come to operate as a 'regime of truth' here and now?' (Foucault, 1990b). This orientation to thinking about knowledge and its relationship to disciplinary power brings with it the expectation that multiple orientations to knowledge, and multiple knowledges, will circulate simultaneously and that some of these knowledges will be subjugated while some will be so self-evident as to operate as regimes of truth. Yet while this account of knowledge has a degree of currency within the project team, not all team members agree with it, or they might acknowledge it intellectually but not appreciate its practical value.

For some members of the project team or in some aspects of the project's work there may be some unassailable truths or certain knowledges about which truth claims might tactically be made. For instance, the right-ness in principle of equal opportunities for and treatment of gay, lesbian, bisexual and transgender (GLBT) people can be seen as an absolute truth of the UK's equalities legislation as proposed in the Single Equalities Bill (CLG, 2007). Here the foregrounding of legislative reform is seen to further cement the status of formal political structures and their underpinning principles (a regime of truth?) as well as the insider citizen who is extended the 'right' to participate in these. In turn, it is also seen to cement the outsider non-citizen who is denied this participation as well as the illegitimacy or even unspeakability of any alternative models of social and political organisation or change (Burgess, 2008). Furthermore, there is a growing body of scholarship and activism that argues that legislative reform actually benefits those who are already most privileged and not those minoritised groups who are held up as its key beneficiaries. This is because such moves only arise when the demands of minoritised groups converge with the interests of the dominant group, even if these interests are simply in terms of having been seen to be 'fair' (Bell, 1992; Delgado, 1995).

Key to these critiques is the point that ideas that circulate as unassailable truths – whether this is that GLBT people should have the same rights as heterosexual people, or that heterosexuality reflects or is the result of normal development, or that sexualities (whether homo or hetero) are the natural qualities of individuals – are in fact constituted as truth through their circulation as true. To notice this movement across orientations to knowledge in the work of the project is not to argue that all claims are of equal value, even if they are irreconcilable, or to argue that some sort of reconciliation should be sought or that one set of ideas should be prioritised over others. It is a reminder that within a Foucauldian frame ideas are indivisible from power. All ideas are positioned, including the idea that knowledge can or cannot be certain, and we can move tactically between these orientations, keeping sight of their promises and costs.

Versions of the subject: constituted and unitary

A Foucauldian account of the subject suggests a subject continually in the making, constituted and reconstituted a subject in and through mobile relations of productive power, 'a form of power which subjugates and makes subject to' (Foucault, 1982:212). This, for Foucault, is the process of subjectivation (Foucault, 1988b, 1988c). This is not a subject who 'is,' but a subject who is 'as if' s/he 'is' (Butler, 1990, 1991, 1993). This subjectivated subject is simultaneously made and made understandable through prevailing knowledges that offer accounts of the subject. Prominent and prevailing amongst these accounts are versions of the cognitive, emotional and moral development of the abiding, unitary, self-knowing subject. Widely accepted in science, education and popular culture, these accounts of the subject operate as regimes of truth and in so doing obscure their claims to greater legitimacy or self-evidence than alternative accounts. Indeed it is the profound productive force in education of, for instance, developmental accounts of the child that Foucauldian work draws our attention to (Slee, 1995; Harwood, 2006). This is not to deny the profound psychic and social reach of the subject who 'is' or the prevailing, silent demand for speech and action to be the work (and the intentional work) of the subject who 'is'. While some of us, sometimes, understand the subject (and ourselves) conceptually to be constituted, we are constituted as *if* we were abiding subjects and so we are continually compelled to constitute (and perhaps experience) ourselves as abiding, unitary, self-knowing subjects. Indeed, such a self is often (perhaps always) demanded in order for the subject to be intelligible. It is no surprise then that we find ourselves taking up these subject positions again and again.

For some members of the project team (note these self-contained subjects whom I can't help but call up here) and in some aspects of the project's work – for instance when taking up a diversity discourse to argue that heterosexuality should not be the only legitimate sexual subject position that children encounter in primary school – this subject position, and the subject who makes the claim, may well be unitary, abiding, the result of developmental processes, self-knowing, even self-evident. That is, as we suggest to the children, parents, colleagues and the media that GLBT people should be recognised as legitimate and full members of a diverse community we inevitably constitute ourselves and others as *if* we were already enduring GLBT and hetero subjects and that we can say with some certainty 'who' these sexualised subjects are (Butler, 2005). These are constitutions of unitary subjects that are likely to have implications in and for a project that was conceived with the problematics of such constitutions in mind.

And Tango Makes Three

Given the ongoing focus of the media on the story books that have been used in project schools, I want to use one of these, *And Tango Makes Three* (Parnell *et al*, 2005), to consider further the knowledges and subjects that circulate in and are constituted through the *No Outsiders* project. *And Tango Makes Three* is the story of two male penguins who form a relationship and together incubate an abandoned egg and rear the chick. This is a tale about penguins but, in the tradition of such children's stories, these are anthropomorphised, given human characters, emotions and engagements. So while it's a story about penguins, it is also a story about people. *And Tango Makes Three* does not name these male penguins in terms of sexual identity or in stated contrast to approved, hetero relational forms. Yet the story does locate the coupling of the two male penguins as unusual in its contrast to the rest of the penguins' male-female couplings, and as unnatural in as much as the egg is abandoned (by a 'normal' male/female penguin couple) and so donated to the male penguins by their Keeper, blessed by this donation. The male penguins' incubation of the egg and rearing of the chick cites heterosexuality, monogamous adult coupling, homemaking and the rearing of young as the coveted prize of couplings entered into by enduring, self-evident, natural subjects. It is a tale of sex in the context of emotional attachment and in the context of normative family relations.

In this sense the book can be read as a relatively conservative inscription of enduring unitary subjects and the normative heterosexual nuclear family, even as it asserts the legitimacy of a homosexual emulation of it. While these might be gay penguin daddies living the dream, this representation of gay life as 'just like' straight life risks, amongst other things, being implicated in disavowing lives that do not look like an ideal (and idealised) hetero-monogamous nuclear family and contributing to this idealisation. Furthermore, as Judith Butler (1991) has argued, this is an emulation that will always fail, given that the homo is the necessary Other of the hetero. Yet at the same time the book does render intimate same-sex relationships and same-sex parents and families visible, intelligible and legitimate. And when it is used in primary classrooms as a storybook and a basis for discussion and further creative work the book makes these subjects visible, intelligible and legitimate in a place where they have been invisible, unintelligible, and illegitimate.

It is not the case that either one or other of these readings of *And Tango Makes Three* and its citations, inscriptions and effects is correct or more compelling or worthwhile than the other. Nor it is the case that one can be made to erase the other – the first reading cannot be extracted from the second in any straightforward way. The book is part of a performative politics *and* it is part of a citational chain that inscribes heteronormativity. This, it seems to me, is unavoidable; we cannot close down one or other meaning. The trick then, is to be aware of what practices might do and to think tactically about their multiple effects.

Media citations

This reading of *And Tango Makes Three* is in stark contrast to readings of the project represented in the media. I do not have space to go into these in detail here: there has been extensive local, national and international media coverage throughout the project's lifetime – much of it controversial. But I explore some of the ways the media has headlined some of the books used by the project and the implications of these forms of representation.

> *Observer* 11 March: 'The Prince married a man, and lived happily ever after: religious groups attack circulation of books raising gay issues among primary school pupils' (Asthana, 2007).

Daily Mail 11 March: 'Four-year-olds will get gay fairytales at school: Schools are teaching children as young as four about same-sex relationships to comply with new gay rights laws' (Clark, 2007).

Members of the project team have had very mixed responses to and readings of the way the media has represented the project, and there is a great deal of potential for analysis. As my colleagues in the project know, one effect these media articles had was to remind me of the queer bubble formed by the community and university contexts that I inhabit, as well as its fragility and the ease with which this bubble is rendered illusory by the force of the discourses that prevail in the world outside it. While the phantasmic, fleeting, or constrained nature of this queer bubble does not undermine its significance or deny its promise, these headlines remind me of the enduring power and knowledge networks that locate and limit it.

The force and endurance of a discourse of naturalised, unitary, self-knowing subjects can be seen in references in these headlines to princes, children and four-year olds – each a self-evident category with which we are all familiar. The force and endurance of a discourse of childhood innocence and risk of corruption is made explicit in the *Observer*'s headline report that 'religious groups attack' and the coupling of 'gay issues' and 'primary school children' in which 'primary' underscores the child-ness and so prior innocence of these children. The *Daily Mail*'s repetition of 'four year-olds' and 'as young as four' constitutes this tethering together of childhood, innocence and risk of corruption even more powerfully. The force and endurance of a discourse of the normative heterosexual nuclear family runs across these headlines pieces, the *Observer*'s parodying of the Princes' marriage to each other cites the proper institution of heterosexual marriage. And the enduring performative force of the erasure of homo-desires and pleasures and containment of homo-subjectivity, even when this is a (failed) copy of the hetero-, underpins the *Observer*'s facetious 'happily ever after' as well as the *Daily Mail*'s reductive 'new gay rights laws' which calls up the derisory discourse of the 'loony left' and 'political correctness' as it denies a legitimate homosexual subject-hood.

All of these discourses are called up by just these two headlines, sometimes explicitly and sometimes implicitly. Butler (1997) stresses that discourses do not have to be expressly cited in language, representation, or practices in order to have constitutive force – she insists that silence, what is not said, can be powerfully constitutive. The constitutive force of silence and the capacity for discourses to be called up in silence is evident in the productive force of the two headlines.

In a context where sanitised and heterosexualised versions of homosexuality are acceptable only as long as they 'are not anywhere near my children,' a sentiment implicitly expressed by the concerned mothers interviewed on BBC Radio 4 (2007), the inclusion of a text such as *And Tango Makes Three* in a primary school curriculum can be seen as a powerful practice of troubling simply in its speaking the legitimacy of same-sex relationships and parenting. And the take up of diversity discourses – recognition, equal opportunities and equal treatment (even when these calls for recognition and equality inevitably inscribe the sorts of natural, abiding, self-knowing GLBT subjects that post-structural accounts have challenged and queer politics have troubled) – comes to appear an important tactical option when the alternative being powerfully promoted and constituted as reasonable by the media is the erasure of these subjects. And given the need to be recognisable in order to act (Butler, 1997, 1999b), these unitary subjects might not be escapable, and in the context of this sort of media coverage we might not want to escape them.

Childhood innocence

A notable absence in the project, and one that is sometimes underscored by the project team, are the sexualities or (perhaps proto-sexual) bodily pleasures of children. The project team recognised this absence and the force of the discourses that create it, and held a specialist academic seminar to explore the issue in September 2008, supported by the Society for Educational Studies. The popular press became aware of the seminar and misrepresented and attacked the work of the project once again (Doughty, 2008; Khan, 2008; Nicks, 2008).

Much has been written about the abiding tension in discourses of childhood between the child's natural innocence and the child's innate potential for wickedness. These discourses insist on the 'natural' innocence of children and their need to be protected as well as their need to be reigned in, correctly trained and socialised in order to guard against

45

the risk of wickedness and protect against their corruption, a task that has been associated with the emergence of mass public education (Aries, 1962; Cunningham, 2006). Just as Eve has borne the responsibility for corrupting Adam and precipitating the Fall from the Garden of Eden (Purkiss, 1994; Warner, 1976), so the already-corrupt homosexual or homo-sympathetic teacher, who like Eve is often female or feminised and carries the responsibility of sexual continence and the risk of sexual incontinence, may corrupt the child she is charged to properly educate and protect.

Education scholars such as Debbie Epstein and Richard Johnson (1998), Emma Renold (2005), Mary Jane Kehily (2002), and Mindy Blaise (2005) have demonstrated the refusal of childhood sexuality in school discourse and the policing of sexuality in practice as well as children's engagements and investments in sexuality practices. In contexts framed by discourses that refuse recognition of hetero-sexualities amongst children, it is unsurprising to find an absolute refusal of homo-sexualities amongst children. To speak of even the possibility of the existence of childish sexualities and pleasures risks their recuperation and redeployment in discourses of precocious sexuality, corruption, mal-development, pathology and abuse. These discourses have incredible force. They are sedimented at the core of the codes and practices of professions from teaching, social work and child health to children's entertainment. They circulate seemingly constantly through popular culture as it is expressed in multiple commercial forms, as well as in social and family life. And this sedimentation is assured through the apparent impossibility of countering these discourses that are sealed and assured by their own truths – to appear to counter, challenge, dispute or disrupt these 'truths' is, by default, to risk constitution as the aberrant Other whom these discourses delineates and guards against.

Some of us have spoken of an abiding tension between the political and theoretical conviction of the correctness of the project's work and the discomfort of talking about these issues with children, while others have spoken of a straightforward and uncompromised comfort with the project work. These different positions and, importantly, emotional experiences seem to indicate less a divergent set of moral frameworks and more a divergent set of discursive frames, some of which we draw on

46

explicitly to conceive of and understand our work and some of which are spectres that haunt our work and which we sense and see only fleetingly.

Politics, tactics, movements

Writers such as Derrida, Foucault, and Butler have identified forms of and spaces for resistance and in my previous work I have examined students' and teachers' practices in school in order to explore the possibilities, as well as the limits, for taking up these forms and spaces of resistance in education settings (Youdell, 2004a, 2004b, 2006a, 2006b). These tactics look to deconstruction and the potential of misfire (Derrida, 1974), discursive resistance and practices of self (Foucault, 1990a, 1990b) and performative politics that shift meaning and or allow discourses into contexts where they have been disallowed (Butler, 1997). Through these previous analyses I have shown how students and teachers are already engaged in performative politics in their everyday practices. If these ordinary, everyday practices are to be translated into a post-structural political pedagogy (Youdell, 2006b) they are likely to look towards and for:

- ■ troubling the normative constitutions of schooling, including the subjectivities of children/young people and students/learners

- ■ creating conditions in which what/who is intelligible/unintelligible might be shifted

- ■ offering young people tools to deconstruct their social and educational locations and redeploy the discourses that locate them

- ■ opening up spaces for children's and young people's practices of self to be intelligible and legitimate

- ■ mobilising and proliferate young people's everyday resistances

As I noted at the start, these post-structural ideas and the political tactics that come out of them are not the only way of thinking about knowledge, subjects or politics in the *No Outsiders* project. Alongside and perhaps over and preceding these ideas are commitments to Left-liberal reform and GLBT identity politics and the knowledges and subjects that underpin them. These commitments suggest a different set of concerns and approaches, including legislation and policy influencing and enactments, curriculum and community recognition, representation and tolerance and diversity and equalities agendas.

Perhaps a better fit for thinking about these sorts of concerns and how they might be pursued is Michael Apple's (in press) reinvigoration of the notion and practice of the organic intellectual. Apple suggests a series of tasks for such a scholar-activist, including engaging in political action where spaces for this open up, facilitating the work of educators engaged in political struggle, developing counter-hegemonic education and acting alongside existing social movements. Although the underpinning philosophies, approaches and even the goals of post-structural, Left-liberal and identity politics differ, they do share a commitment to challenging the enduring and normative privilege of particular social groups constituted in particular ways, a sense of the important part that education sites can play in enacting these challenges and a recognition of the significance of everyday practice inside classrooms.

I am not arguing that a particular political philosophy, approach and set of goals should be pursued and others set aside. Rather I want to argue that we analyse the possibilities and limits of particular philosophies and approaches, including the risks that one approach may have for the goals of another. This analysis, however provisional and uncertain, might offer insights into possibilities, limits and risks as well as tactics. Michel De Certeau (1988) draws a useful distinction between the strategies of institutions and governments that are encoding in policy and legislation and embedded in the structures of institutions and the tactics of everyday life which people deploy, often tacitly, in order to survive and make the best of their daily existence. These tactics do not need to remain oblique, although they often do. As an everyday politics in education we might engage in an ongoing process of analysing the potential of our tactics and the multiple effects of the tactics we deploy. In the face of different circumstances and demands, and in pursuit of particular effects, we might deploy politics of opposition, recognition, resistance, deconstruction, reinscription, and performative practice. We need not be fully conscious of our tactics in order for them to have effects. But when they are elaborated and critically interrogated we are able to consider the forms they might take under particular conditions, even when the 'right' tactic will remain undecidable and we know that we cannot guarantee effects.

Foucault's ongoing participation in political activism that included state-focused protest alongside his intellectual work underscores the fact that his attention to the productive effects of micro-power ran alongside his engagement with the continued significance of sovereign power and the need to engage at times in acts of political resistance to this (Foucault, 1988b). Similarly, Butler's direct work with the medical and mental health professionals who assess transgender people presenting for gender reassignment, alongside her philosophical work on the illusory nature of gender, demonstrate her recognition of the need for intellectual work and pragmatic, practical politics (Butler, 2004). Furthermore, Butler's (2007) concern with the possibilities for new collectivities to be formed to act in the face of the disciplinary and coercive forms of power that are seen in the US and UK military interventions in Iraq illustrates again the need to articulate the post-structural and the Left.

Allowing post-structural and critical Left politics to co-exist and speak to each other in the way that I think both Butler's and Foucault's writing and practice suggests also reminds us that a turn to post-politics is not simply an identity politics pursued through the practices of self of an individualised subjectivated subject (although Foucault clearly saw this as part of political practice). Rather, it reminds us that individuals are always constituted in and through relations of power and practice in discursive fields that are inflected by and constitutive of the cultural and the material. Butler's thinking about new collectivities invites us to think again about social movements, how these develop, how they can be supported and the place of educators and scholars in them. The demise of the popular left, a move away from oppositional political philosophy and the sedimentation of neo-liberal individualism seem together to have led us to neglect or stop being concerned with social movements. The ideas I have explored here indicate, for me, that this may well be the moment to revive the idea of and our commitment to social movements, bringing together new collectivities in mobile ways, complete with potentially irreconcilable ways of thinking and for hybrid purposes. Indeed, we might think of the *No Outsiders* as approximating a moment of such a new collectivity.

4

'Vanilla'[5] strategies: compromise or collusion?

David Nixon

In contrast to the explorations offered by Youdell and Cullen of the affordances and foreclosures of 'queer' within the project's work, Nixon offers an alternative critique, again emerging from the intersections within the project between queer and gay rights discourses. Using interpretive lenses drawn from critical explorations of sexualities equality and sexual geography (from which he draws the chapter's framing concepts of 'safe space, troubled space and dangerous space') he focuses on the ways in which discourses of the 'acceptable homosexual' and fear of moral outrage may have led project members to make their strategies of intervention and resistance altogether too safe. He explores the effects and impacts (or lack of them) of these 'vanilla strategies' and examines what happened when the project was suddenly perceived as sexually dangerous. Nixon considers the implications for the project's participants, and the wider educational world, of moving from safe to dangerous spaces.

Introduction

From its beginning, the *No Outsiders* project has worked within twin frameworks roughly described as equalities/social justice/ human rights on the one hand, and on the other the exploration of queer in terms of theory, pedagogy and curriculum. This chapter considers the intersections, challenges and tensions between these frames via three concepts: 'vanilla' as defined by Silverstein and Picano (1993) to mean safe and approved sexual practice and fantasy, Rofes' (2000) contention that lesbian and gay educators have abandoned anything other than vanilla in order to be acceptable in the teaching profession, and Bell and Valentine's (1995) process of mapping sexual geographies. Using project literature, interviews, field notes, project website discussions, blogs and media reporting I describe space which is safe, troubled and dangerous, concluding that while the project has been queerer than at first sight, the risks of this engagement have also been highlighted.

in his article 'Bound and gagged' in the journal *Sexualities,* Eric Rofes speaks about attempting to negotiate the boundaries of acceptable behaviour between the worlds of some contemporary gay (predominantly male) cultures and the culture of the educator. Rofes asks:

> Are there ways to situate ourselves [as educators] in relationship to activities common to some contemporary gay cultures such as cyber sex, drag, sex in parks or participation in leather subcultures, without denying our own interest or participation, feeling shame or being ejected from our profession? (2000: 442)

He concludes by emphasising what has been lost:

> We've made compromises and sacrifices that have gone unspoken and unacknowledged. We've gained limited entry into the classroom by denying authentic differences between many gay men's relationships to gender roles, sexual cultures and kinship arrangements compared with those of the heteronormative hegemony. (*ibid*:459)

These issues have been present in much discussion and reflection during the second year of the *No Outsiders* project, coming starkly into relief as a result of reactions both within the project and in the media to a day seminar entitled 'Queering the Body: Queering Primary Education'.

Located in English primary schools, this participatory action research seeks, as its introductory literature states:

> ... to support you [the teacher researcher] in a creating a positive, inclusive ethos and challenging homophobic discrimination in your own school or classroom. This might involve, for example, including non-heterosexual relationships within discussions of family, friendship, self or growing up, exploring a range of identities and relationships through literacy, art, history or drama, or including a specific focus on homophobia within a class- or school-based initiative to tackle bullying.

The project's teacher researchers were provided with reading material to use in their own practice contexts, showing inclusive family structures or challenging gender norms, suitable for the primary age range. They were encouraged to explore this material or discover their own ways of developing this work. An interactive web forum restricted to project team members has allowed teacher researchers and university researchers to share data and reflect on this data both experientially and theoretically.

By the start of the second year of *No Outsiders* the teacher researchers and university researchers felt they had greater confidence and experience. They began to ask questions about the kind of images of lesbians and gay men which were being held up, consciously or not, as models of acceptability. To what extent were we advertising only safe, comfortable 'gay families'? Did we include any images that might threaten or disrupt this pseudo-nuclear setup? Were we pursuing a vanilla approach out of strategic necessity, as a first step, or out of reluctance, fear or doubts about queer? Was this compromise or collusion with the heteronormativity we all recognised as so prevalent in schooling? If we did things differently, what would a queer primary project look like? This chapter begins to answer these questions, as well as exploring what happened in terms of public media reaction when the project explicitly opened up the domain of queer.

In theoretical terms, the project situates itself and its research within the broadly postmodern perspective by which sociologists of education and their colleagues in related disciplines examine gender and sexualities. The work of theorists such as Foucault, Derrida, Sedgwick and Butler are then interpreted into the more specific arena of education. Foucault's (1970, 1997a, 1998) analysis of power, resistance and sexualities demonstrates the constructed nature of classifications hitherto taken for granted, the networks of power which operate in and create the discourse of sexualities and the possibility of individual and group resistance within a network of power relations.

Butler's notion of the 'heterosexual matrix' or 'heterosexual hegemony' (1990, 1993, 1994) describes the density of practice and concept which allows autonomy to a single sexual culture; however, she points out that that which is maintained by constant repetitions and appeals to antecedent authority can also be disrupted by the development of new 'echo chains' and fresh appeals. Postmodern and post-structuralist writers provide, therefore, the means to examine the 'taken as read,' the commonsense normalcy of life in and around schools, revealing who or what is omitted from a reading and the far from normal experiences of minorities. The insights of queer theory are particularly significant (Jagose, 1996) in relation to education. Sumara and Davis write, 'Queer theory does not ask that pedagogy becomes sexualised, but that it excavate and interpret the way it already is sexualised – and, further-more, that it begins to interpret the way that it is explicitly hetero-sexualised' (1999:192).

Bell and Valentine examine how 'the spaces of sex and the sexes of space are being mapped out across the contemporary social and cultural terrain' (1995:1). By discussing the intersection of the discipline of geography with contemporary work about sexualities, they are able to trace growing interest in how space is sexualised and how sexual identity is inscribed on both bodies and landscapes, advocating a queer reading of geography as well as a queering of space. It is by means of the trope of space that material in this chapter is organised: Safe space, Troubled space, Dangerous space.

Safe space

In some senses, the introduction of books like *And Tango Makes Three* (Parnell *et al*, 2005), *We Do: A celebration of gay and lesbian marriage* (Rennert, 2004), and *ABC: A family alphabet book* (Combs *et al*, 2000) into the primary staffroom and classroom marked a huge step forward in the promotion of sexualities equality. Although *We Do* and *Tango* tend to show safe gay families, it was only twenty years ago that UK legislation included a clause (the infamous Section 28 of the 1988 Local Authorities Act) stating that 'a local authority shall not ... promote the teaching in any maintained school of the acceptability of homo-sexuality as a pretended family relationship,' which was only repealed in England in 2003. The children's book *Jenny lives with Eric and Martin* (Bösche, 1983), a particularly anodyne version of domestic harmony, was reputed to have inspired the clause. But even the 'safe' texts offered to project schools were not safe enough for some: the head teacher of one project school locked the books in her office, only allowing circulation of *The Sissy Duckling* (Fierstein and Cole, 2002) on the condition that the blurb on the inside cover containing the words 'gay' and 'safe sex' were pasted over. Rasmussen (2006) recognises that the challenge of these kinds of text lies in the description of straight and gay relationships as equal and similar; this is more discomforting than equal but different, which still allows an escape into the myths and stereotypes of othering.

The provision of safe space in the classroom for the teaching of diversity has a number of facets: if teachers are not comfortable saying words like gay and lesbian, then unease will be quickly communicated to children, which will tend to reinforce already established negative associations. Gay and lesbian teachers have a particular interest here if they intend to risk being more open about their own sexualities; and children with gay or lesbian parents will talk less openly about their own families if they feel unsafe to do so. An example of the benefits of this safe space linked to the reading of a project text is given in one account of a classroom incident:

> One child in Class One – reception age [4-5 years old] – told the class her carers were getting married – both female. This provoked huge discussion, mainly the other children saying this was impossible and the class teacher then came to me and asked me for support. So I went in and read *And Tango Makes Three* and showed them the pictures of civil ceremonies in the photo book we were sent. They all laughed, but I decided they would have laughed if I'd told them butterflies used to be caterpillars. Anyway, they loved the story and then the little girl whose foster parents are (allegedly) about to get married stood up and explained the bedroom situation in their house. (Not quite sure why she decided to announce this, but you know what reception children are like.) Something along the lines of: there's Anne's bedroom with the computer and there's the bedroom they sleep in together and my bedroom is next to that one. All hands went up at this point and I thought, here we go, but in fact they all wanted to say where their bedrooms were in their houses in relation to their parents. It was fun! There was a parent helper in the room and I asked her afterwards how she thought the session went and she was really positive about it. (Sue, web posting)

This account also illustrates some awareness in very young children of a complex concept like 'getting married.' One child realised that it was possible for a same-sex couple; the rest of the class felt that this was problematic. The introduction of bedroom arrangements does not lead to a conversation about gay sex, but to a comparison of the geography of children's houses. This undercuts both objections to the research that primary aged children are too young to understand this kind of teaching and adults' obsessive link of 'gay' with sexual practice.

For older children something different is possible. Andy had already come out to his class with some trepidation earlier in the year, and now recounts the benefits:

> After summer I was talking with a mixed group of Y5 and 6 children over lunch. We were talking about pizza. One girl said to me 'Does David like pizza?'
>
> Me: (I was stumped for a second) 'David?'
>
> Girl: 'You know, David! Your boyfriend.'
>
> I have had thousands of conversations with children over the years about the weekend or a holiday and my partner David has remained invisible, referred to as 'my friend' if at all. Once I came out and told children my partner was called David, he suddenly became real. To have a child ask innocently about him in a conversation was wonderful. And there was no reaction from the other kids. I said he did like pizza and then the conversation moved on. A great moment! Heterosexual people are able to mention their wives and husbands and partners, now I do too. As teachers and adults we are modelling all the time the behaviour we want the children to reciprocate. I no longer feel I am modelling fear and hiding. (Andy, web posting)

Beyond Andy feeling a warm glow of acceptance, there is evidence here of normalisation. Perhaps more significantly, Andy discovers that to say nothing about himself does not imply a neutral space but rather conveys to children the underlying connotation of gay sexuality as something to hide, to be fearful of. Now gay sexuality is something to talk about, or not to talk about, in the dynamic of an ordinary conversation.

Troubled space

These accounts are examples of the gains to be made, in terms of supporting diversity, from the adoption of vanilla strategies. As a tactical approach to persuading critics, encouraging supporters, and publicly reversing two decades of silencing, they should not be underestimated. However they are problematic in at least three ways. They perpetuate the distinction between 'acceptable' and 'unacceptable' sexual sub-cultures enjoyed by gay (and straight) men and women, aspects of which are summarised in Rofes' words above; they do not reflect more generally the life experiences of men and women today and they do not reflect the theoretical milieu in which the project is situated.

Rofes' first statement above does not suggest that children should be given tours of bars, parks, and gay bath houses/saunas and tearooms/cottages, though that is what the project's critics have imputed (see 'Dangerous space' below). Rather, he highlights continuing tensions between teachers' roles as agents in a process of cultural reproduction which seeks to normalise and validate an almost exclusive and narrowly constrained heterosexual matrix and teachers' free expression of their sexuality in the diversity of its desires and (be)longings. How to live with this tension has both personal and professional consequences, with the threat of both shame and dismissal if too bright a light reveals private lives to a prurient public (see Patai, 1992 and DePalma and Atkinson in press, for concepts of surplus visibility). Rofes suggests that this tension and fear prevent the interrogation of prevailing family structures and their implication in heteronormative discourses; we fail to recognise the diversity of families which fall outside these narrow norms and to learn from what non-traditional families have to offer.

Where Rofes' statement is less helpful is in its reluctance to challenge the conflation between lesbian, gay, bisexual and transgender (LGBT) people and sexual activities, which has been remarked upon in research elsewhere (eg Nixon and Givens, 2004; DePalma and Atkinson, 2006). In the context of the *No Outsiders* project, for example, the use of a photo of two muscled young men in shorts and singlets with a young child that was selected by project teachers as an image of gay parenting has been interpreted in one primary school as showing gay pornography. Such conflation accounts for neither the range of heterosexual practice which includes cyber sex, drag, sex in parks (UK English: 'dogging') and sex parties (UK English: 'swinging') nor the range of homosexual practice which includes long-term, monogamous, committed and loving relationships. The heteronormative hegemony behind these conflations gains some of its strength from the system of hierarchical pairs described by Derrida (1974). The first term in binaries such as man/woman, mind/body, straight/gay is associated with power, rationality and the presence of a transcendental order, while the second term marks absence, the 'hidden, forbidden or repressed' (Bass, 1978:x). Contrary to the assumptions of the popular press, a queer primary pedagogy would not be concerned with the minutiae of gay sex: its aim might be the far more disruptive one of upsetting the authority of these pairings. If Andy can talk of his boyfriend in the classroom without essentialising his own sexuality, then this disruption will have started.

Spivak (1988) uses the term 'strategic essentialism' in her work on race theory to refer to the option of allowing discrete and essentialist categories to persist temporarily, while recognising their limitations, because an overall strategic aim is advanced. By failing to acknowledge the rich and subversive multiplicity of the lived experiences of the twenty-first century adults our young people will become, there are hints of this essentialism in the work of the project. Again the rationale may be that fixed sexual identities which include a valorisation of 'gay' may be difficult enough at primary level without speaking about greater fluidity or a queer identity; additionally, a robust approach to prejudice and discrimination may be facilitated by a more fixed version of identity. There is always the possibility that denying identity equals denying persecution: the fist, the boot or the knife-blade do not first ask questions about ontology. Nevertheless, there is a risk of reifying both homo- and hetero- identities through knowledges and normalised images which are partial and distorted, and this continues to construct the binary pairs on which much discrimination is based (Talburt and Steinburg, 2000). This is not to suggest that people choose to be gay, straight, bisexual and so on; rather that the way in which they choose to describe themselves and which others choose to describe them may vary across time, geography and culture. And such choices will have differently valued consequences.

It is this more general point which would be a possible starting-point for the classroom, with pupils who already experience a variety of familial structures.

The *No Outsiders* research endeavour situates itself within a postmodern and post-structural perspective which informs much contemporary academic discussion of sexualities. To use this plural form is a result of an understanding of a fluidity of identity by contrast to an essentialist and fixed sexual identification. The project takes particular note of Judith Butler (1990, 1993, 1997) and her accounts of gender and sexuality, including her notion of 'degrounding': that shifts in understanding or practice may occur when we stand in two places at once, or do not know exactly where we are standing (Butler, 1994; see also Atkinson and Brace, 2007; Atkinson and DePalma, 2009).

The concept that we perform our gender and sexuality every day in different ways is taken up by Deborah Youdell, who insists that what is performed in one particular way – ie in a way which is antipathetic to sexual minorities – may indeed be performed differently and in ways which trouble normalised identity constructions. She discovers 'the discursive practices that students deploy in order to resist performatively constituted wounded identities and (potentially) reinscribe themselves *again differently*' (Youdell, 2004:481, original emphasis). As a research team we also recognise the potential impasse between this theoretical approach and a lively embracing of issues of social justice. We bridge this gap by a call on the works of feminist post-structuralists in education like Glenda MacNaughton:

> Feminist poststructuralists believe that in order to disclose which discourses should be privileged it is important to have a clear analysis of how discourses are structured, what power relations they produce and reproduce and the implications of different meanings for social relations. (2000:56)

Similarly, Elizabeth St. Pierre writes of her 'deep, ethical concern for the damage done to those trapped in the everlasting, insidious grids constructed by prevailing power and privilege' (St. Pierre, 1997:282).

One project member highlighted that 'the intersection of a multiplicity of identities within myself does not stop me from making judgments about how those identities interact with the everyday world' and that within the life of one individual such identities may at any one time be mutually contradictory (Elizabeth A, web posting). This suggests that postmodernism does not represent a tidy replacement structure, but rather attempts to reflect the messy complexity of identity which is a particular characteristic of sexual identities, including the possibility of advocating for greater equality.

This overview makes clear the presence of creative tensions between theory and practice at the heart of this research. We are aware that we risk collusion in failing to disturb sufficiently the settled normalities of accepted hetero- and homosexual practice, so we are uncomfortable that we may have inadvertently settled for the compromise of strategic essentialism. We still wish to see changes in school practice to support sexualities equality, so on occasions we have to come to that compromise. What evidence is there from within project schools to illustrate these methodological and philosophical tensions? The two incidents described above in which primary-aged children unpack the realities of family life in twenty-first century Britain may be read in a much queerer way. Several myths are exposed here: it is possible to talk about gay and lesbian people in primary school lessons without sensationalising, and without reference to sexual activity; a male primary teacher having a same sex partner of whom he speaks in the classroom is not an 'impossible body' (Youdell, 2006a); support staff and parents are sympathetic to the teaching of equalities, especially in relation to homophobic bullying. This last challenges the notion that such work is simply extreme political correctness imposed by left-wing academics on local cultures (see Wardrop, 2009).

Two significant events within our project schools also suggest that we are more queer than at first sight – something to reassure those who wish to settle for neither compromise nor collusion. The finale of an inclusion week in a small village school took place in the local parish church. The children processed a rainbow flag into the church and acted out the story of *King and King* (De Haan and Nijland, 2000) in which two princes fall in love and marry each other. The priest in his homily at the end referred to Jesus as supporting outsiders:

> Actually, there was another person who was really, really into *No Outsiders* as well. It may come as a big surprise to you who that person was. See Jesus was really into *No Outsiders* as well. He always went to look for the people who were on the edges (excerpted from videotape).

This juxtaposition of young children, gay symbolism and story and a religious institution in its medieval glory troubles a number of discourses: in addition to those about children and sexuality, assumptions about the prejudices of religious faith are also disturbed.

In another school, a teacher used the theme of alternative fairy tales to dress up and act out a lesbian Cinderella, complete with boots, sparkly wig and leather jacket, allowing children to question her in character about her 'girlfriend.' She had previously read *King and King* and found that some children still wanted to insist that the prince really wanted to marry a princess. While the pupils deployed some energy in either returning the story of male characters to the hetero-norm or refusing to shift Cinderella from her pretty, white straightness, others took permission to unsettle the comfortable fixity of this story and explore queer alternatives. The teacher herself, given that this was almost a coming out performance of her own, began to re-inscribe what it meant to be a primary teacher (see Chapter 2 and Chapter 5 for analysis of this event).

Dangerous space

If these developments mark a shift in some primary schools from vanilla to queer, then limits and brakes were imposed at the end of the project's second year. The project team ran a university seminar entitled 'Queering the Body: Queering Primary Education' and publicised its intentions on a number of academic and professional websites:

> One of the most fundamental questions the research team has been addressing since the start of the project concerns the problematics of the body. The team is concerned to interrogate the desexualisation of children's and teachers' bodies, the negation of pleasure and desire in educational contexts and the tendency to shy away from discussion of (sexual) bodily activity in *No Outsiders* project work. Through ongoing debate and exploration during the project, members of the project team have challenged the pervasive images of romantic love and life-long monogamy portrayed by the lesbian and gay characters in the children's books used in project schools; have questioned the denial or repression of their own sexual identities, pleasures, desires and investments; have explored the underpinning cultural and religious discourses which banish sex from sexuality; have raised the need for and purpose of strategic essentialism in relation to sexualities and gender identity; and have challenged each other to go beyond imagined possibilities into queer practice. In addition, the team has explored the multi-layered ways in which sex/gender/sexuality are written on and performed through the body through the repetition and appropriation of specific social and cultural codes and symbols; and ways in which such performativity might be interrupted/disrupted in order both to queer the norm and normalise the queer (excerpt from seminar announcement).

Putting aside the political advisability of placing in the public domain what might be conceived of outside academic circles as particularly problematic, the focus of these seminar papers was to explore precisely what this essay highlights about the methodological tensions and potential contradictions which have been spoken, unspoken, or alluded to tangentially across the project almost from its inception. The interest here is not in the contents of this seminar (to which its participants responded with enthusiasm), but in the reactions it generated and what these reactions tell us about attitudes to sexualities in primary schools. We are not too far again from Rofes' cyber sex, drag, sex in parks or leather subcultures: troubled spaces become dangerous spaces, but dangerous for whom?

Initial negative reactions came from teachers engaged with the research who, spotting the possibility of misinterpretation, were worried and angry lest hard work and success in their own primary schools would be undermined. After some discussion, teachers were reassured, perhaps most effectively by one project teacher who planned to participate in the academic seminar. The reaction in public media was not so measured. The *Daily Mail* of 16 September ran the headline 'Teach 'the pleasure of gay sex' to children as young as five, say researchers', and opened with the words:

> Children as young as five should be taught to understand the pleasures of gay sex, according to leaders of a taxpayer-funded education project. Heads of the project have set themselves a goal of 'creating primary classrooms where queer sexualities are affirmed and celebrated'. (Doughty, 2008)

While the phrase 'the pleasure of gay sex' is the newspaper's own, elsewhere the article cleverly quotes from the seminar description and intersperses comments, including those posted on the Christian Institute website:

> The discussions provoked a furious reaction from critics of the homosexual rights agenda. Simon Calvert of the Christian Institute said: 'When an adult who is working in a primary school suggests that children should explore their sexuality, that should result in a complaint to the police'. Patricia Morgan, author of studies of family life and gay adoption, said: 'The proposal is that primary school classrooms should be turned into gay saunas. This is about homosexual practice in junior schools. The idiots who repealed Section 28 should consider that this is where it has got them.' (*ibid*)

Similar stories appeared in the *Daily Telegraph*, with the headline: 'Primary schools 'should celebrate homosexuality'' (another invented quotation) (Khan, 2008) and in the *Daily Star* with 'Outrage at gay sex lessons for kids, five' (Nicks, 2008). Blogs in each of these newspapers followed the same line. Several right wing websites also reported this story, for example: 'BNP Leader Calls for Funding Cuts to State-Sponsored 'Gay Sex to Five Year Olds' Researchers'; the same sites named some of the researchers (one by means of an unauthorised entry into a social networking site) and were linked to other sites and blogs which called for 'Capital Punishment for the Paedo-Intellectuals'.

As a result of this reporting, individual teachers and researchers were distressed, anxious and not a little fearful, with support being called on from local authorities and university security departments as well as from friends and family. At a major project dissemination event, initially planned as the project's publicity launch, the decision was taken not to invite press representatives. Specific schools and teachers were not named, and a sense of a celebration of achievements was harder to sustain than would otherwise have been possible. This media coverage, alongside the earlier reporting of protests over the project's work in two Bristol schools, may lead other schools and heads to question whether the cost of this equalities work is too high both professionally and personally to justify the risk. This view has not been helped by an otherwise sympathetic report in the *Times Educational Supplement* under the headline 'Gay education in primaries climbs back into the closet' (Brettingham, 2008). While numerous messages of support came from the project's allies around the country, those not already familiar with its work may have taken away the impression that to emulate it would be dangerous and somehow corrupting.

At a level of theory and practice, significant lessons may be learnt from all this. There are familiar strategies deployed: the reduction of education about homosexuality and sexualities equality to the simplistic, undefined notion of 'gay sex' through reference to censured sexual practices, raising the spectre of the 'dangerous queer' of the 1980s New Right agenda (A Smith, 1994); an attack on public funding bodies by invoking the image of the hard-pressed taxpayer, again reminiscent of a previous era; the deliberate conflation of homosexuality and paedophilia; the undermining of teachers' professional judgements about age-appropriate pedagogy; and the disassociation of education about sexualities equality from other diversity strands. Behind these strategies lie discourses of hetero-patriarchy and child protection which suggest through a quiet but potent elision that only with a traditional system of values and judgements are children safe, or in reverse, that by upsetting the traditional order you risk the safety of your children. The physical threat behind this manoeuvre is revealed in one of the blog headlines ('Capital Punishment for the Paedo-Intellectuals'); associated threats to professional status and public reputation are just under the surface. The link to conservative Christian organisations invokes an attack on the cosmic order and the possibility of wider moral chaos should such equalities work continue (Holloway, 1980).

This feels like dangerous space for researchers and practitioners alike, but dangerous too for children. The project literature already described writes into the curriculum and the life of the school the presence of same-sex families, thereby ending potential feelings of invisibility for these children and families and also promoting awareness of the notion of difference for all children. The outlawing of homophobic bullying, and of indiscriminate and pejorative use of 'gay' protects all children, when this behaviour is used often to highlight and castigate any child who is different from a narrow norm. The safeguarding of children may not be best accomplished by reliance on the concept of a golden age of childhood innocence (see for example Renold, 2005).

The resilience of these powerful and toxic alliances should perhaps not have surprised the project team, but the degree of investment in notions of childhood innocence bears further investigation. The concept of queer is still not understood widely, or perhaps remains frighteningly fluid: bisexual, transgender and queer identities are perceived as being too much for the primary school. Gay or straight in their essentialised forms are less upsetting, but beyond that is forbidden territory – vanilla with a twist?

Returning to Rofes' (2000) article, I would argue that his concerns about assimilations and trade-offs are still helpful as spotlights to pick out the detail of our practice in schools and institutions of higher education. *No Outsiders* research has begun to engage in a queerer pedagogy, and a queerer reading of what we have already achieved, as the examples described above suggest. The team has not avoided the exploration in childhood discourses of 'desire, bodies and erotic practices' that fail to disrupt 'sex as an effective form of social control' (*ibid*:459) or, as one of our university researchers phrases it, investigating 'the performative force of silence' (Deb, web posting). But we are now more fully cognisant of the risks and recuperations involved.

Notes

5   'Like the ice cream of the same name, it's both popular and plain. Used by some in a merely descriptive way, and by others pejoratively, "vanilla" refers to a person whose sexual fantasies and actions are among the most socially approved both in the gay world and by those straights on its periphery' (Silverstein and Picano, 1993:208).

5

Speaking the unspeakable in forbidden places: addressing lesbian, gay, bisexual and transgender equality in the primary school

Alexandra Allan, Elizabeth Atkinson, Elizabeth Brace,
Renée DePalma and Judy Hemingway

This chapter explores the ways in which the unspeakable – the recognition or expression of non-normative gender and sexual identities usually silenced or foreclosed in primary education contexts – has not only found deliberate expression in previously forbidden contexts in the course of the project, but has also seeped out into a range of arenas within and beyond the project's schools. These themes are developed further in this volume through Atkinson and Moffat's examination of the effects of lesbian and gay visibility in educational contexts in Chapter 7, and Nixon's exploration of safe, troubled and dangerous spaces in chapter 4. Here, three scenarios are examined in three different project settings: the staffroom, the classroom and the after-school club. The authors explore the implications of leaky knowledge and its impact on the shaping of discourses of knowledge both within and outside the school.

Introduction: the production of school as a heterosexual place

The primary school is often thought of as a place of safety and innocence (Kehily and Montgomery, 2004; Renold, 2005; De-Palma and Atkinson, 2006); a place where childhood is nurtured and sheltered, and where attempts to address what are seen as 'adult' issues may be seen as intrusions into or threats to this safety zone. In this context, lesbian, gay, bisexual and transgender (LGBT) identities are made absent in one sense through the fact that they are not addressed in formal school contexts, while being made doubly present by the fact that they are taboo, and are brought into being through the popular discourses of homophobia.

This chapter draws upon data generated in primary schools to interrogate the ways in which school is produced as a particular bounded place (or collection of places) where sexuality, and particularly non-heterosexuality, is carefully policed by these boundaries. Since September 2006, the *No Outsiders* research team has been exploring ways of addressing LGBT equality in the context of English primary schools. Each teacher researcher has generated strategies in their own practice context, with the support of university-based research assistants, and as strategies and issues emerged they have been shared with the wider research team.

Massey writes of the spatial in terms of complex geometries of power; 'Since social relations are inevitably and everywhere imbued with power and meaning and symbolism, this view of the spatial is as an ever-shifting social geometry of power and signification' (1994:3). Drawing upon students' own metaphors, Gordon and Lahelma (1996) compare school to an ant's nest, with spatial relationships and movements carefully channelled, compartmentalised and specialised. Yet as McGregor has noted, schools are not static self-contained entities but institutions continually being produced by interconnecting relationships and practices which extend in space and time (2003:253). Drawing upon field notes and journal entries recorded by teacher researchers and research assistants, we investigate the ways in which this power-laden social geometry of school has been meaningful within our project, by focusing on three very different school places: the classroom, the staffroom and a school-based after-school art club. Our analysis engages with the contingency of place-making to show that place is neither a unitary experience nor a neutral stage upon which social relations are enacted.

The classroom: dissident bodies in (hetero)normative landscapes

This vignette explores the intermeshing of the space of the classroom and the place of the body in a provisional reading of an alternative fairy tale performed during a primary school literacy-hour project. The narrative focuses on how the body of a lesbian Cinderella challenges the (hetero)normative landscapes of pedagogic spaces. It is with the politics of the sexualised teacher body, framed within the wider 'power-geometries' (Massey, 2005) of the British education system, that this tale begins.

Producing lesbian space

> The only thing that me and Cindy had in common is that we are lesbians and I guess neither of us would really want to dress like Cinderella but I would never wear what Cindy wore so I created a character fairly different from myself. (Laura, *No Outsiders* teacher researcher)

In her initial year as a class teacher who is not 'out' to the eight- and nine-year-olds she teaches, Laura faced a range of issues. For example, within the space of the government-imposed daily literacy hour she was motivated to explore the themes raised in the gay-affirmative story books loaned to participating schools. Laura's determination challenged her deputy head and parallel teacher, whom she eventually 'managed to persuade,' and her teaching assistant who regularly removed the age-appropriate project books from display by putting them in a cupboard. Having passed the gatekeepers, Laura recorded in her research journal, from which the following quotations are taken, her resolution to 'plan a unit which looks at ways that the themes in fairy tales can be changed and adapted'.

The scheme of work during the ensuing fortnight began with the well-known alternative tale of *The Paper Bag Princess* (Munsch and Martchenko, 1982). This princess not only defies convention by refusing to dress as pronounced fitting by a prince but also confounds the heteronormative denouement of other tales by rejecting the prince himself. Although Laura reported that her class 'loved' this overturning of the masculine privilege of self-determination, She recorded that the pupils were 'finding it hard to understand why princesses might not want to wear beautiful dresses etc!' In the next activity, Laura directed pupils to write as the Paper Bag Princess to Cinderella, 'giving her advice'. This was followed by work on the more recently published *King and King* (De Haan and Nijland, 2000), and mention of homosexuality. Laura wrote:

> I talked quite openly with my class about the Princes' sexuality – we began the lesson with a letter from the Prince asking the class for help (because he has to meet all these princesses but doesn't want to marry any of them) and then we read the book.

Despite this discussion, the embeddedness of heterosexuality and ideas about marriage were such that the reasons Laura's pupils suggested for the prince not marrying a princess cohered around his preference for singleton status and his wish to avoid gold-diggers. *King and King* was also used as the stimulus for pupils to write lonely hearts advertisements seeking a partner for the gay prince. With the exception of two pupils, the class accepted the protagonist's sexuality and wrote of his wishing 'to meet a handsome Prince to go on adventures with, play chess with, etc.' At the end of the book when the prince marries another prince, Laura observed that most pupils 'did not react negatively to the outcome,' although mention of lesbians evoked laughter and cries of 'yuk!'

During the next literacy hour, Laura briefly left the classroom and re-turned as Cindy. Aware of the limitations of restrictive forms of lesbian identity and body habitus, she observed:

> I found it difficult to decide what kind of Cinderella I would be. I didn't want to be completely feminine because they see loads of very feminine fairy tale characters all the time and yet they also seem to think that all lesbians look like men so I wanted to challenge that in them too. So I decided to be de-finitely female but not pink and pretty. I wore boots and a sparkly wig and a skirt and a leather jacket.

Resisting the Cartesian mind/body dualism associated with traditional storytelling, Laura performed an alternative Cinderella story which was 'a lot of fun up to the point at which I was telling them about this girl I met at the party' whereupon 'it was very scary'. Recalling that 'we've talked in class about gay men – far more than lesbians (how does that always happen?!),' Laura felt on 'pretty new ground'. After the per-formance, Laura's class hotseated Cindy (asked Laura questions which she answered in character as Cindy). Laura reflected on this experience:

One boy asked, incredulously, 'So, are you really gay?' and for a moment my heart stopped (this was getting somewhat too close for comfort but I had set this whole thing up and had to go with it) – so I answered 'Well, this is my girlfriend so yes, I'm gay' and pointed to the picture I had of this girl on the interactive whiteboard. That felt horrible but I couldn't avoid it, seeing as I was perfectly happy about answering all the other questions and I was doing this for the very reason that I was aware that we hadn't spoken much about lesbians ... so I wanted to present a positive lesbian to them who was comfortable about being a lesbian.

Again resisting same-sex relationships and perhaps other aspects of Cindy's lifestyle, the pupils asked 'Will you get married?' and 'When will you get married?' Laura felt that the pupils thought 'the story hadn't been finally completed until there was marriage!'

Despite the production of lesbian space, Laura felt that she had 'no idea' what she would do if asked directly about her sexuality. But, she argued, 'even though I can't do it yet, I feel children need to know that there are lesbians teaching them, existing in classrooms with them every day.' Laura concluded by writing:

Yes, Cindy did come and share a classroom with them for a little while and they interacted with her and she obviously challenged some of them who assumed she was straight but then she went away. The episode perhaps hinted at a different way to perform gender and sexuality and presented the children with an alternative they'd not considered and I think this, combined with other things we have done, is all contributing to them developing different understandings but, in itself, it's not enough.

This vignette portrays the body itself as the site of meaning-making, as 'the irreducible locus for the determination of all values, meanings, and significations' (Harvey, 2000:97). This particular body, 'caught up in a system of constraints and privations, obligations and prohibitions' (Foucault, 1977:11), serves to illustrate what kinds of bodies are prohibited from the primary classroom. It has been argued that the 'desexualisation of teachers as teachers' is attributable to 'the desexualisation of schooling required (however problematically) by government and dominant sexual culture'. Epstein and Johnson, 1998:122). Simultaneously, however, desexualisation assumes default heterosexuality and while heteronormative teaching bodies are openly displayed in the domain of the school, lesbian bodies tend to be rendered invisible. In this example, one *No Outsiders* teacher researcher challenged taken-for-granted heterosexuality and produced a lesbian space (Valentine, 1996) in the classroom by using 'representation, gesture and play' (Creed, 1995:102) in the creation of an alternative Cinderella.

Pedagogic authority and the politics of hope

Laura's analysis of her lesbian Cinderella performance echoes Davies' view that 'it is not enough' merely to expose pupils to stories without guidance in deconstructive skills (Davies, 1993:138). From a similar position, it has been posited that as teachers we should not 'abdicate our pedagogic authority' (McDowell, 1994:247) by neglecting to assist children in understanding that certain authorial voices are more worthwhile than others. Rather, as 'directors of conversation' (*ibid*:242) teachers should arguably take responsibility for helping pupils to recognise sexuality and thereby work towards greater social justice. More recently, an argument in support of 'directive' teaching approaches has been pursued to affirm the moral legitimacy of homosexuality (Hand, 2007:69). The emancipatory potential of adopting directorial strategies, combined with greater awareness of the power-geometries of place and space, can be deployed by pedagogues to help children 'read against the grain' (Davies, 1993:138) of the moral traditionalism typical of the fairy tale genre and involve them in the making, re-making and if necessary re-making again of space (Harvey, 2000) and place in all their myriad forms.

The staffroom: border patrol

If, as McGregor (2004) suggests, little research has focused on the spatiality of education and the ways in which social relations constitute and are constituted in these spaces, it seems that even less research has focused on the constitution of staffroom space. Notable exceptions, however, have focused on the ways in which power arrangements (especially gender relations) are constituted and spatialised in the place of the staffroom (Shilling, 1991; McGregor, 2003; McGregor, 2004; Paechter, 2004b). This chapter goes on to explore the ways in which sexuality and sexual identities were performed in the staffroom and how many teachers felt restricted to talking about sexualities equality in these spaces – often viewing them as fixed and bounded places and the only safe, private and respectable (adult) places for this work to be addressed.

All schools participating in the *No Outsiders* project received a set of selected books and resources which affirmed LGBT identities and troubled gender stereotypes. As the project books and resources packs were delivered to the schools they were usually unpacked on staffroom tables and left for teachers to browse at their leisure. The staffroom functioned as a sort of border patrol through which these items passed on their way to the rest of the school, and sometimes this border passage was denied. For some schools this has been a strategy demanded of teachers by governing bodies, where, until further staff training has been carried out, the books and any conversations relating to the project were expected to remain in the staffroom. For other schools this has been a decision made by senior management teams; some suggesting that the project needs to stay within the space of the staffroom so that the teachers can 'get to grips with it first' in order to examine their own 'prejudices as a staff' before 'working out ways of moving forwards'.

The staffroom as a private space

A dominant way in which the staffroom appeared to be characterised in these schools was as a 'private' space. McGregor (2003) uses Rose's (2002) research to demonstrate how spaces like the staffroom are often used to extend people's private lives out from the home; that personal photographs and cards are displayed in these spaces in such a way that they extend space-time beyond the limit of the room and constitute it as familiar, familial and intimate. The next section is based on the experiences and reflections of one of the authors, a *No Outsiders* research assistant, and is written in the first person.

From my own observations in school I could certainly see the way in which the staffroom was used for private chatter, gossip and general relaxation, as the following field notes demonstrate:

I was told upon arrival at school today that this is a particularly nice school to work in, mainly because the staff are so friendly but also because the staff are extremely supportive of the project work and are quite open about sexuality – discussing it in an open-minded and unprejudiced manner on a daily basis. Despite having been told this I am still surprised at the level of personal chatter that plays out in this space and the (apparently) comfortable way in which the staff ask each other about their weekends, their partners and their latest

73

'famous crushes' whatever their presumed/acknowledged sexual orientation. This feels like a very different space to the classroom that I have just left – much more intimate, friendly and relaxed.

Yet despite this apparent ease and comfort with talking about sexuality among colleagues in the staffroom, what many teachers felt less comfortable about was the idea of these conversations leaving this 'private' space and entering a more 'public realm'. In some schools this was a particular concern about parents, often because it was feared that they may 'go even more public' and let the media know about the work in school. However, this was also a concern about the information entering the private space of the home (and people's minds) after it had entered 'public space'. As Brickell's (2000) research suggests, this is not an unfounded fear, for the idea that lesbian, gay and bisexual people 'flaunt' and 'promote' their sexuality and as such force their ideas onto other people, invading their private thoughts and spaces, is a dominant one that is regularly rehearsed in the media. As Brickell notes, ideas like these can be traced back to the work of Freud enabling a perception of the mind as a series of spaces that are open to being territorialised, invaded and polluted.

Because of the distance from the children, parents and governors, the staffroom also appeared to be characterised as a 'safe space' – a space where the project and other issues regarded as relating to (homo)sexuality could be discussed away from potential outrage, violence and prejudice. In some of the schools I visited I was warned about the use of 'more public' spaces in the school, such as the playground – about how pupils and their parents would become agitated and aggressive towards members of staff. It is also no wonder that some teachers tried to keep their discussions of (homo)sexuality bound to these 'safe' spaces, for as Skeggs (1999) suggests, fear of violence is as significant a factor in people's use of space as violence itself. Within schools teachers are often expected to take responsibility for their own safety, and so if visibility (being recognised as LGBT or an ally) is a central means for instigated attack, then invisibility would appear to be the safest option. Indeed, a number of authors have commented on the need for 'safe' spaces for LGBT people. Hubbard, in particular, contends that given the fear of homophobic abuse, the metaphor of the private space of the closet appears to be an 'appropriate description of the schizophrenic spatial lives that many gays 'not out' in public space lead' (Hubbard, 2001:56).

The staffroom as an adult space

In other schools the concern with the project 'leaving the staffroom' was much more related to concerns about the innocence of children. In this sense, the staffroom was often characterised as a particularly 'adult' space where issues of sex and sexuality could be discussed away from prying eyes and ears. There is a large body of literature that acknowledges the way in which childhood has been viewed as a time of 'presumed sexual innocence' – a time where children are presumed to remain untouched and untroubled by the cares of the adult sexual world to come (Jackson, 1982; Piper, 2000; Renold, 2002; Kehily and Montgomery, 2004; we also recognise that this notion is raced and classed, see Epstein, O'Flynn, and Telford, 2003). As Jackson (1982) suggests, discussions of children and sex remain controversial (especially in schools); children are defined by adults as a special category of people deserving adult protection and sympathy. Sexuality is seen as a 'special area of life' and one that should be reserved for adulthood. Through observation I noted a marked difference in the way in which issues relating to the project – and particularly the words 'sex' and 'sexuality' – were talked about in the staffroom and how they were discussed in the rest of the school. I reported this observation in my fieldnotes:

> As I am walking through the main corridor of the school today after break time I suddenly begin to realise how stilted our conversation about the project has become. This appears to be in direct contrast to the flowing and 'intimate' chats that we were having in the staffroom just minutes ago. Words like 'sexuality' and 'gay' are now being muttered as opposed to being stated confidently and I am aware that I too begin to follow the teacher's lead – I too begin to mention the project in hushed tones and become constantly aware of the children who surround me.

The way in which many of these teachers drew on dominant discourses of childhood innocence is not a new finding – many teachers continue to struggle with these ideas (especially given the confusion that Section 28 still holds for many). What is interesting however, is how these relations constituted and were constituted by social space; the ways in which the school corridors, in particular, were being recognised as public, mobile, child-inhabited and therefore, dangerous spaces to talk about sexuality (McGregor, 2004).

Staffroom space as fluid and dynamic

By being asked to keep (or to attempt to keep) homosexuality in the staffroom, teachers were arguably being asked to try to maintain the dominance of heterosexuality within the school. As Skeggs (1999) proposes, it is essential to see these claims to space simultaneously as claims to identity. On an everyday basis the heterosexualised nature of the school space often went unnoticed – many teachers were unaware of the ways in which heterosexuality was spoken about or continually performed in the 'public' space of the school, in the music that they played in whole school assemblies, in books they read to their classes and the conversations they had in lessons about their wives or husbands (see Binnie, 1997; Bell *et al*, 1994; DePalma and Atkinson, 2009).

Nevertheless, there were many times when the project and wider discussions about homosexuality or homophobia could not remain in the staffroom, but were outed through incidents of homophobic bullying in the playground or through children's own discussions about their lesbian parents. There were also times during the research where the 'safe' and 'private' nature of the staffroom space could be questioned. This was not just limited to those who identified as lesbian or gay, for in one school a female teacher who identified as straight felt too intimidated to talk about the project with others in the staffroom. This example perhaps confirms Skeggs' (1999) point that even if space is heterosexualised it does not always benefit all heterosexual people.

Neither schools nor their staffrooms are spatial and temporal islands, and so for effective sexualities equality education to take place in schools we need to take account of these flows and networks that begin and end outside the staffroom and the formally accepted space of the school.

After-school clubs: a shift in time

Massey argues against 'a view of place as bounded, as in various ways a site of authenticity, as singular, fixed...' (1994:5) and suggests that space and time work together in the creation of social space (and her notion of space in terms of 'envelopes of space-time' usefully reflects this). In the instance of the after-school club described in this vignette, classroom space literally changes in relation to time, and formal rules and relationships change also. This transformation, we argue, offers teachers huge potential for exploring sexualities equality.

An exploration of identities and labelling within the informal space of an after-school art club, as part of the *No Outsiders* project, opened up possibilities for discussing sexualities with year six primary school children. This initiative focused on the Holocaust. It was facilitated by a class teacher, a *No Outsiders* teacher researcher (Kate) and visiting artists and writers.

Bringing 'gay' into the primary classroom

The session described here focused on labelling. It included eighteen children, the class teacher and Kate, and was also observed by a *No Outsiders* university researcher. This session was one of three after-school art club sessions held in addition to several formal classroom sessions exploring marginality and difference in the context of the Holocaust.

The children were initially asked to consider different 'outsider' words (for example 'gay', 'Muslim', 'disabled'), and symbols (for example the LGBT rainbow flag, the Muslim sickle moon, the wheelchair signifying 'disabled'). Kate and her colleague then led the class in a discussion about the way in which such labels are used in injurious ways (for example using the words 'gay' or 'Paki' as insults), and in positive ways (for example gay people and Muslim people using labels and symbols to identify themselves and having pride in these identities). Finally the children were asked to choose a symbol or label to decorate so it was attractive and positive.

So the session explicitly focused on the forbidden subject of sexualities, albeit embedded within wider discussions around identities and marginality. Teacher researchers throughout the *No Outsiders* project, and especially their colleagues, have expressed concern about discussing sexualities within the classroom. They fear parental and wider public reaction, and are specifically concerned about how to introduce sexuality as an appropriate classroom subject. As we saw, the fears are partly induced by the notion that schools are havens of childhood innocence. Through the explicit discussion of sexualities Kate brought in to the primary classroom not just the forbidden subject of sexuality, but also the doubly forbidden subject of LGBT sexualities, situating LGBT oppression alongside other oppressions and actively breaking the customary silence on sexualities within such settings.

Coming out

One aspect of the session was to look at certain words that are used as terms of abuse and why they are offensive. For example, Kate asked the class how her Muslim colleague might feel if she were called 'Paki' and followed this by asking how she herself might feel if she were called 'gay,' as she *was* gay. This was the first time that this teacher researcher had come out to children and she described the experience like this:

> It was a very important moment for me, and while I have never been hidden, I have not felt I could come out before now ... Coming out had to be something that happened in an appropriate context, and this was exactly right. Before the session I had thought I would say I was gay, but was not entirely sure. I used to teach this class, so felt at ease with them, and they with me. In fact, not teaching them now (except in art club) made it easier.

As Epstein and Johnson (1998) have highlighted, 'out' gay and lesbian teachers are threatened with the loss of their credibility, homophobia, adverse media reactions, loss of privacy and even (in the past at least) of their jobs. As discussed earlier, teachers' personal sexual lives are not seen as an appropriate subject in classroom spaces, despite the fact that heterosexual teachers are implicitly and explicitly 'out.' Arguments suggesting that LGBT teachers refrain from discussing their relationships within the school fail to acknowledge that children themselves might benefit from the openness of LGBT role models for a variety of reasons: because they may identify (or eventually identify) themselves as LGBT or just 'different,' because they have gay or lesbian parents (Letts and Sears, 1999; Kissen, 2002) and because one of the duties of school is to prepare all children to live in a diverse society (DePalma and Jennett, 2007).

Safe spaces

The researchers in the project have spent much time exploring how it might be possible to make safe spaces in which children can talk about sexualities and difference, including the sexualities of their parents, their parents' friends or indeed themselves. This vignette shows that the informal space of this after-school club appeared to operate as just such a safe space for Kate to discuss her own sexuality. She described this in the following communication:

> Coming out to the art club was easier, and a considered decision. It's true that it's more relaxed, as we all are there by choice ... if things had gone wrong, or caused a much bigger reaction – I didn't have to stand up in front of them all day every day for the rest of the year! I think this also let them be freer with me, as there was not going to be a change of role to a more formal relationship the following day.

The informal nature of the space was a significant factor in Kate's decision to reveal her sexuality to the children. The formal-to-informal shift that takes place in the transition between school hours and after-school hours is associated with the relaxing of formal teacher-pupil relationships. With the blurring of boundaries between public and private, a space is opened up in which it becomes possible to explore sexualities (including teachers' sexualities) – a subject usually relegated to the 'private' sphere. As Epstein and Johnson argue, 'schooling stands rather on the 'public' side of public/private divisions, while sexuality is definitely on the private side' (1998:1).

This moment of coming out appeared to open up the space in which children themselves could talk about same-sex relationships in safety. hooks (1994) argues that teachers must talk about themselves in the classroom before expecting children to do likewise. Kate reflected:

> Their reaction made me feel very accepted and supported by them. Even [a] boy who had described gay as 'minging'[6] wanted to be sure I knew that he didn't think *I* was [disgusting].

Early on in the session, this boy had responded to the word 'gay' with 'that's minging' and one of the girls had challenged him by suggesting that there wasn't anything wrong with being lesbian or gay. However, it was only later, when Kate revealed her own sexuality, that the girl mentioned that she had an aunt who was gay. The conversation then snowballed: another girl said she knew a number of people who were gay (friends of her parents) and that it upset her to hear them insulted. Finally, the boy told the class that other people called *him* gay and, significantly, when the children were later asked to take an outsider symbol and decorate it, this boy chose the gay and lesbian pink triangle. Kate was positive about the effects of the project for this boy:

> The father's been in to talk to the head teacher to say 'I'm worried, my son's a fairy and what on earth am I going to do?' The father's at the stage where

it's just not acceptable, surely not *his* son, which is why this kid has got a hard road over the next few years ... But hopefully, I know it'll be a very small thing in his life really, but to have this little bit of work where we're saying it's OK, he can at least think 'well not everybody thinks the same way, and there are people who think it's OK.' And it'll be really important for him as well if his peer group is saying 'well that's all right, there's nothing wrong with that'.

As Epstein *et al* (2003:20) suggest, 'a whole range of behaviours can be labelled 'gay' when a boy does them,' and this session (and the project more generally) allowed this boy to tell others that this issue was affecting him.

Leaking

As Massey suggests (1994), 'place' is not fixed and its boundaries are porous. Although this session took place within the boundary of the classroom, its effects clearly went beyond it. The teacher researcher describes the way in which her coming out had effects that leaked beyond the classroom and wider school walls:

The word must have spread throughout the school, but I have not had any comeback, nor has it been reported to me by any staff. I did however hear from a couple of parents of children who were in the session. They described their children as 'buzzing' when they came out of the session. One parent, who had her daughter when in a lesbian relationship ... said it had prompted a very meaningful conversation between them about sexuality and relationships.

The fear articulated by several of the *No Outsiders* teacher researchers that parents might be offended or upset by the discussion of sexualities in primary classrooms is here countered by positive parental reactions. And the session prompted a 'meaningful' discussion between one child and her mother that might not have happened otherwise.

In effect, talking about sexuality in this context represented talking in the 'public' realm about what is usually considered 'private'. However, it might also be argued that together with the informal nature of the after-school space, this discussion of sexuality transforms this public space into private. Seemingly paradoxically, this constitution of the private then leaks outwards via discussions between parent and child into the public world outside of the classroom, yet simultaneously into the private world of the family. Thus the public and private boundary appears to have a permeability that challenges the notion that sexuality is necessarily contained in one sphere or another, and the notion that there is indeed such a boundary.

Conclusion: Deconstructing mind/body, public/private ... school/life

Massey (1994) usefully makes the link between place and nostalgia. This resonates with the notion, critiqued here, of childhood place as historically innocent and free of adult (sexual) concerns. As Paechter argues, 'Because schooling is obsessed with the exclusion of the body, its explicit introduction is highly threatening' (2004a:317). However, '... the body and its sexuality are both ubiquitous and marginalised within schools' (*ibid*:309). Whilst sexuality is supposedly absent in the primary school classroom, it is also strongly present both *through* that absence and the implicit presence of *hetero*sexuality. As Epstein and Johnson (1998) argue, children are schooled into gender and sexuality in school settings that are suffused (Epstein *et al*, 2003) with sexuality that is, specifically, a heterosexuality. This is seen in the *hetero*sexualised fairy-tales that children are asked to read, the casual conversations held by staff about their heterosexual husbands and partners, and by the way in which, as Paechter (2004a) suggests, children learn about their sexua-lised bodies via their separate use of boys' and girls' toilets and chang-ing rooms.

Nevertheless, as Brickell (2000) suggests, spaces have not been seen as singular or *a priori* for some time now. Researchers have investigated the ways in which children have been able to territorialise and re-territorialise a number of traditionally accepted 'adult' spaces (K Ras-mussen, 2004). They have questioned the possibility of determining safe and violent and spaces (Skeggs, 1999) and explored the possibilities of 'private matters' entering 'public spheres' (eg gay and lesbian pride marches, Brickell, 2000). Many social geographers have followed Massey (1994) in suggesting that space and place needs to be seen as dynamic and multiple, extending beyond a singular context or place.

And so, despite the fact that our own perceived 'private' spaces can come to take on a material existence that we truly believe in, spaces can never really be fixed, for their boundaries are always open to con-tinuous struggle and they are continually being made and remade through social relations (McGregor, 2004). For schools in particular (Nespor, 1997:xiii), the division of space into the public and the private is never helpful, as it enables wider problems (such as homophobia) to be simply seen as school problems and it does not account for the ways in which education and learning (about issues like homosexuality and alternative family forms) could (and does) take place 'through constellations of relations that extend well beyond the classroom' (McGregor, 2003).

Massey writes that place is defined by social relations that spill over boundaries:

> The particular mix of social relations which are thus part of what defines the uniqueness of any place is by no means all included within that place itself. Importantly it includes relations which stretch beyond – the global as part of what constitutes the local, the outside as part of the inside. Such a view of place challenges any possibility of claims to internal histories or to timeless identities. (1994:5)

Vignettes like these and others show how the *No Outsiders* project as exemplified by has offered insight into the potential of consciously and persistently working across these apparently boundaried spaces within and beyond schools: the project leaks from the staffroom into the 'dangerous' spaces of the school corridor; it leaks inwards from teachers' own convictions and actions into the classroom, and outwards again to the community; it leaks from the pages of the project books to the homes and workplaces of project teachers' colleagues and friends and it leaks back and forth between participating teachers' private and professional lives, with the project teachers finding themselves performing actions in ways – and in spaces – in which they would never have thought possible.

Inspired by the learning potential created by these conscious border crossings, we exhort educators deliberately to reflect on the spatial geographies of schools and deliberately to transgress them. One of the most fascinating and productive aspects of the *No Outsiders* project has been simply noticing boundaries and mapping the various micro-cultures of different places in the school: the classroom, the corridor, the playground, the staffroom are all interrelated yet bounded. These observations have inspired us to consider some important questions.

What is acceptable and unacceptable to say and do? What happens when words and actions leak from one space to the other? What happens when we open new channels and allow the fully diverse and physical world beyond school to trickle into our carefully restricted school spaces? How can this be done so that spatial transgressions are productive while at the same time safe enough so that we don't lose our jobs?

Simply asking these questions is a first step, and testing them is a great stride. We might consider letting lesbian and gay identities, usually reserved for the staffroom (if anywhere), leak into classrooms. We might discuss our own or friends' civil partnerships when we discuss marriage or civil rights, we might all refer to our partners as partners, rather than husbands, wives or 'friends', and engage in discussions with children about why. We might bring sexualised language from the playground into assemblies to unpack the meanings and implications, rather than allowing it to flourish unchallenged in the less adult-centred school spaces. We might invite our own and children's physical bodies into school, with all their complexities of sex, gender and sexuality, and we might discuss how and why these complexities are policed in certain ways, and in some cases entirely erased, inside and outside school. Overall, we think the critical and persistent practice of boundary mapping and strategic leaking can be at least as effective in advancing sexualities equality in schools as any specific resources or curriculum guidance, and that this practice requires teachers to develop new ways of thinking that enable them to identify and question established school geographies.

Notes

6   Slang term indicating disgust.

6

Toys, pleasures, and the future[7]

Susan Talburt

As a guest contributor to this volume, Talburt takes an outsider's view of the issues and possibilities raised by the work of the *No Outsiders* project. She offers a close examination of the reproductive futurism in which pedagogy for social change is embedded, and makes it clear that 'queer', with its rejection of hetero-sexuality's linear future and of the idealised notion of the Child for whose better future we are exhorted to strive, cannot operate within such futurism. She suggests that a queer pedagogy in this sense is an impossibility, particularly as queer recognises and validates the sorts of human activities – notably pleasures justi-fied in their own terms and not aimed at a future end – which reproductive futurism rejects. In her play on the possibilities of pleasure, and on the pleasure of (un)imagined possibilities, Talburt offers a challenge to members of the project team and to others working within the tensions between ends-based social justice work and the uncertain troublings of 'queer.'

Let me start with a story. We might call it a playful, pleasurable story, as it is about toys. The story comes from a recent issue of a corporate gay magazine, *The Advocate*. Thumbing through it one day, a headline caught my eye: 'Sex toys and children make uneasy bed-fellows'. It seems that a company called Adam Male, which identifies itself as a distributor of 'the highest-quality sex toys, bondage gear, adult DVDs, and sex accessories for the gay market' (Lisotta, 2008) and which donates over 25 per cent of its profits to philanthropic causes, sought to give money to the wrong organisation. According to the article, 'On April 8, Adam Male released a statement announcing it was adding the

85

safe-schools advocacy group Gay, Lesbian, and Straight Education Network (GLSEN) to the list of charities to which it donates profits' (*ibid*). When contacted by *The Advocate*, GLSEN's director of communications disavowed knowledge of the donation, stating that GLSEN had 'not received any funds from this organisation, and we do not accept any unsolicited corporate sponsorships' (*ibid*). Well, *The Advocate* was not to be deterred and pressed further into this important story. A phone call revealed that Adam Male's parent company, PHE, reported that its check for $250 had indeed been cashed. Not to let the story end there, the Advocate recontacted GLSEN, whose communications director now responded that although the check had been cashed, GLSEN would be reimbursing PHE. *The Advocate* ended its story with a coy phrase: 'GLSEN's reticence toward Adam Male may be due to the company's product line, which includes grown-up devices like the Clone-a-Willy Kit' (*ibid*).

This article left me wondering what readers were meant to learn. What problems does Adam Male represent for GLSEN? Why is *The Advocate* so interested in pursuing the ambivalent tale of GLSEN's disassociation from this sex toy company's $250 donation? And why did the *Advocate* not inquire into the corporate citizens GLSEN does deem appropriate? These include such entities as: Citigroup, which helped Enron set up the sham transactions that eventually brought down the company; PricewaterhouseCoopers which worked with Enron and was involved in five other accounting scandals in which it overestimated profits, created misleading financial statements and committed accounting violations; Merrill Lynch, which was involved in stock market misrepresentation and the Martha Stewart scandal; and Merck, which falsely recorded $12.4 billion in pharmacy co-payments that it never collected.[8]

As many who work with lesbian, gay, bisexual and transgender (LGBT) youth know, GLSEN is a non-profit organisation in the US that seeks to legitimate LGBT subjects, both human bodies and bodies of knowledge, in schools. GLSEN embraces a future in which schools will be safe for all students, who should have 'an education free of bullying and harassment, regardless of their sexual orientation or gender identity, or that of their friends, family or loved ones' (Jennings, n.d.). This future-oriented stance points to a past and present that need to be corrected. As the organisation's founder, Kevin Jennings, explains on GLSEN's website,

'We are steadfast in our commitment that, by coming together, we will all play a part in creating a better future for America's students' (*ibid*). GLSEN, then, would heal past and present wounds and prevent possible future harm.

Discomforts of pleasure

I want to hold this story in the background as an entry to thinking about questions of pleasure, institutions, identities, temporality and adult-child relations as they relate to some of the questions-or anxieties-framing the proposal for the 'Education and the Body: Queering the Body; Queering Primary Education' seminar coordinated by the *No Outsiders* project team and funded by the Society for Educational Studies in September 2008, the occasion that brought me into the conversation of the *No Outsiders* group.

A few sentences in the seminar proposal identified tensions between the proposed work and the discourses and practices that came to constitute it:

> The team is concerned to interrogate the desexualisation of children's and teachers' bodies...; the negation of pleasure and desire in educational contexts ...; and the tendency to shy away from discussion of (sexual) bodily activity in No Outsiders project work, including the rejection of references to sexual acts by pupils. (p1)

The seminar proposal asks, 'At what cost do we deny children's and teachers' sexuality? What do we lose if desire and pleasure are banned from the classroom?' (p2). These are difficult questions, particularly as the *No Outsiders* project is supported by and directed to the state and its future and its citizens' futures. It appears that *No Outsiders* dwells in the interstices of seemingly necessary institutional equity discourses and queer challenges to the heterosexual matrix's normalisations. My sense is that this 'placement' is at once productive and impossible.

What I suggest is that the queer inclusion of bodies, pleasures and desires in the space of education confounds 'straight time,' or heterosexuality's linear future (see Freeman, 2007; Halberstam, 2005). This is not only because it tampers with the supposedly natural time and order of the development of innocent children but, more saliently, because it engages schools and children in a temporality that is not oriented to the future on which the heterosexual matrix depends. In short, it is impossible to put pleasure to work for a certain type of future.

Many working in primary education lament what Michelle Fine, twenty years ago called 'the missing discourse of desire' (1988), which she recently identified as 'still missing' (Fine and McClelland, 2006) and to which Tobin (1997) and others have added the term 'pleasure'. The elision of sexuality, pleasure, bodies and desire in schooling is said to protect the child's innocence and to protect it from the spectre of the child molester, a figure conflated with the male homosexual, recruitment and contagion (Sears, 1998; Silin, 1995; Tobin, 1997). Yet this idea of protecting childhood innocence denies children engagement with crucial knowledges, silencing children (and adults) and erasing their sexual agency. This adult and expert discourse of innocence-to-protect has a pre-existing and permanent temporality as something that will evolve naturally to knowledge and experience in 'due time.' As Jenkins argues, 'the innocent child is a myth, in Roland Barthes's sense of the word, a figure that transforms culture into nature' (1998:15). This naturalisation of the myth of innocence, in turn, makes the myth itself appear to be innocent, as if it were not discursively constructed and had no effect of erasing children's sexuality or sexual agency.

Eloquent arguments have been made for the inclusion of pleasure in education – and not only as a challenge to discourses of innocence. Mary Lou Rasmussen argues that the 'deployment of pleasure provides an efficacious departure from educational research that too often re-inscribes pathological stereotypes of lesbian, gay, bisexual, transgender, and intersex (LGBTI) identified young people' (2004, p445). This thinking in the domain of research challenges dominant ideas of 'at risk' gender- or sexual-non-conforming minority youth (such as the representations of GLSEN) and reminds us that danger and the wound are not necessarily minoritised youths' only dimensions. Yet, in the space of pedagogy, it may be that we should not frame pleasure as antidote to wounds and speech as antidote to silence.

As Foucault (1985) pointed out in the second volume of the *History of Sexuality, The Use of Pleasure*, pleasure is not a spontaneous or natural event but, to borrow Erica McWilliam's words, is 'constituted and organised through available discourse' (1999:3). Ethical subjects learn to recognise themselves as what Foucault called 'subject[s] of desire' (1985:6) and engage in techniques of the self relative to proper and improper pleasures. Pleasure, then, constitutes part of the governing of the self, in which subjects perform work on themselves as part of the process of changing the self. This self-creation is constrained by available discourses and by subjects' social, political, geographic and economic positionings. Pleasure is bound up with regulated (including self-regulated) processes of becoming. Yet despite social, cultural and institutional incitements to particular forms of pleasure, this becoming a 'subject of desire' is not easily knowable or understandable. The state and its institutions, as well as informal apparatuses, seek to regulate becoming, pleasure and desire, sometimes through instruction and sometimes through repression.

But as we know, both instruction and repression can be productive of surprises and unpredictabilities. Thus, while pleasure and desire can be thought of in terms of conformity or resistance to the state or dominant moralities, they can also be thought of in more creative terms.

Queer conceptualisations of pleasure place it outside the realm of the political, as a force that we mistakenly tether to purposes, however liberatory our intentions. Elizabeth Grosz, for example, writes of

> a refusal to link sexual pleasure with the struggle for freedom, a refusal to validate sexuality in terms of a greater cause or a higher purpose, the desire to enjoy, to experience, to make pleasure for its own sake, for where it takes us, for how it changes and makes us, to see it as one but not the only trajectory in the lives of sexed bodies. (1995:228)

Let me add that if pleasure has no teleology, neither does the sex toy from which GLSEN would distance itself, unless one wants to configure erotics and orgasms as teleological, which I do not wish to do.

Impossible pedagogical pleasures

But what happens when we bring together the non-teleology of pleasure and the teleology of the developing child? What seems to me the pedagogical impossibility of pleasure in schools relates to the oxymoronic idea of 'queer futurity' suggested by Lee Edelman's (2004) provocative text, *No Future: Queer theory and the death drive*. Although he does not name it as such, a 'queer futurity' is impossible. Edelman argues that mainstream politics – and I read this to include any struggle that engages institutions, particularly those of the state – is based on a fantasy of identity and meaning creation. The political centres the future as its regulating force, the ideal that drives subjects' actions. Whether working from the proverbial left or right, we all agree on creating a better world, a better future. Edelman argues that to justify this better future, the political uses the Child (with a capital C to distinguish the figure of the Child from actual children) to regulate the present and what can count as political discourse. In his words, 'we are no more able to conceive of a politics without a fantasy of the future than we are able to conceive of a future without the figure of the Child' (*ibid*:11).

Edelman names this order 'reproductive futurism,' a 'mandate by which our political institutions compel the collective reproduction of the Child' (*ibid*:11). This futurism opposes the figure of the Child to that of the homosexual and queerness generally, which represent the death drive, or 'negativity' (*ibid*:7) threatening the social order by refusing futurism's logic of meaning and identity production. The seeming self-evidence of reproductive futurism preserves 'the absolute privilege of heteronormativity by rendering unthinkable, by casting outside the political domain, the possibility of a queer resistance to this organising principle of communal relations' (*ibid*:2).

This is a Lacanian argument that places the social and political in the Symbolic order, that of signs, representation, language, rules and the law. The order in which subjects are formed, the Symbolic is the place in which the signifier and signified are always separated. This separation of signifier and signified-or lack of wholeness-means that elements in the Symbolic have no positive existence but are constituted through their differences in a field of alterity and absence. As an effect of the Symbolic, the Imaginary order incites subjects to misrecognise the Symbolic as transparent, creating a fantasy of a world in which identities appear as stable, meaningful and recognisable. And the Child becomes the object and subject of the search for positivity, identity. But queerness understands the 'vicissitudes of the sign' (*ibid*:7) and lives where 'narrative realisation and derealisation overlap' (*ibid*, 2004:7). Edelman explains:

> Where futurism always anticipates, in the image of an Imaginary past, a realisation of meaning that will suture identity by closing that gap, queerness undoes the identities through which we experience ourselves as subjects, insisting on the Real of a jouissance that social reality and the futurism on which it relies have already foreclosed. (*ibid*: 25)

For Edelman, then, queerness embodies the Symbolic's unnameable remainder of jouissance, which is more than pleasure and pain, 'a violent passage beyond the bounds of identity, meaning, and law' (*ibid*: 25). It is an acknowledgment of the subject's openness and the impossibility of closure or transparent representation through language. His thinking resonates with Roland Barthes' (2005) distinction between pleasure and jouissance, in which pleasure resides in the domain of conscious enjoyment and linguistic representation (the Symbolic) whereas jouissance is pure affect that does not know boundaries and dissolves subjectivity. Pleasure, then, is contained within the social order and jouissance is within and beyond it.

Given signification's inherently oppressive politics, Edelman's suggestion for queerness is to 'withdraw our allegiance, however compulsory, from a reality based on the Ponzi scheme of reproductive futurism' (2004:4). Futurism's continual attempts to produce wholeness and meaning, to suture past and present to repair the gap, create a perpetually deferred future that regulates our present, holding us captive to its promise by never arriving. Like illegal Ponzi, or pyramid investing, schemes, this is a future based on promises that can never materialise. Rather than submitting itself to the social order's repetitive logic, queerness must take up 'the impossible project of queer oppositionality' (*ibid*:4). This entails accepting the negativity ascribed to the figure of the queer as 'the bar to every realisation of futurity, the resistance, internal to the social, to every social structure or form' (*ibid*: 4). Edelman says polemically:

> We do not intend a new politics, a better society, a brighter tomorrow, since all of these fantasies reproduce the past, through displacement, in the form of the future. We choose, instead, not to choose the Child, as disciplinary image of the Imaginary past or as site of projective identification with an always impossible future. (*ibid*:31)

So this argument asks queerness to secede from the impossible and normalising project of creating future meanings and identities in the name of the Child.

Unteachable subjects

But can queerness refuse the Child in schools full of actual children? Cavanagh asks whether educators could 'embrace a pedagogy opposed to reproductive futurism, normative heterosexuality, and the categorical gender binaries that the latter inscribes' (2007:27). I am doubtful, as that pedagogy ceases to be a pedagogy *per se*. Etymolocially derived from the ancient Greek, pedagogy means 'to lead the child.' To lead implies a destination, to a space, place, time, or self. So even as educators may wish to lead children to open discussions of pleasure, desires and bodies, such a pedagogy tethers pleasure to signification and the Symbolic order's production of wholeness and identity, to liberatory fantasies of a better tomorrow. This better tomorrow may seek to be a different tomorrow, but it is still one that speaks the language of reproductive futurism and its ontological literalism.

Brenkman (2002) critiques Edelman's stance, arguing that the political 'is not simply a mechanism of social reproduction; it is also the site and instrument of social change. Nor is it simply the field of existing power relations; it is also the terrain of contestation and compromise' (p176). Yet, as Edelman (2002) notes in his response to Brenkman, such a stance is unable to disarticulate queer from the very logic of futurism Edelman problematises. In fact, in many instances, as queerness has entered schools, it has tended to function as little more than what Foucault (1978) called a 'reverse' discourse. In other words, it has offered interventions that appear to be oppositional, but that function as tactical elements operating within, and thus upholding, dominant logic. Whether queer or identitarian, many school-based projects enact an insidious queer developmentalism that seeks to respond to heteronormativity's futurism (Janssen, 2008), creating an impossible 'queer futurity'.

If, as Cavanagh describes the myth, 'It is for the good of the child that we censor discussions about the body and its sexual capacities in school' (2007:14), I would turn the question around to ask if it is also for the good of the child that we are incited to discuss the body, desire and sexuality in school? If queerness is to speak of pleasure, desires and bodies in schools, how can it do so without submitting itself to the Symbolic's realm of signification in the name of reproductive futurism? How can it avoid substantialising identities through the ontological literalism of the political order, a substantialisation supported, if not made possible, by the figure of the Child and our collective future? My answer is that it cannot, for attaching political change and subject formation to pleasure works against pleasure's very transformative potential. To return to Grosz's (1995) idea of pleasure as but one of many trajectories, if we consider pleasure as 'desubjectivating' (Sullivan, 1999:252), we cannot centre an intentional, autonomous actor who seeks or creates pleasure with a direction or temporality. Rather, as Sullivan says of pleasure:

> It is a pre-discursive, pre-subjective event, an exposure, a becoming-open that is unnameable, that is, if you like, queer. Pleasure is a transformative process, not because it is something I can employ to my own ends, but because it inaugurates the very site of (un)becoming. Pleasure exists before the question of its meaning, its use, arises. (1999:254)

Pleasure does not develop. It creates and recreates in ways that cannot be known in advance or directed to a future.

GLSEN, which does not refuse identity or the future or the Child, does refuse pleasure, as GLSEN understands the ontological literalism of the US cultural imagination in which children and pleasure have identities and purposes. So GLSEN understands that to accept Adam Male's donation is to align itself with the development of future sex toy and bondage gear shoppers. My sense is that what is troubling is not so much the morality of these aberrant behaviours-though the morality is always an enticing excuse, just as it is easy to point to the sad (tragic) loss of childhood innocence, or development out of time. More troubling is the purposelessness of toys and their pleasures, their orientation to a present and a presence that reproduce nothing. If the sex toy points to a future, it is a future of what Lauren Berlant (2004) calls 'live sex acts,' which do not seek the reproduction of the same, and are not about substantialised identities or appropriate citizenship. Rather, 'live sex acts' is a metaphor for subjects who follow a queer zeitgeist that understands 'sexuality as a set of acts and world-building activities whose implications are always radically TBA [to be announced]' (p77). Schools cannot announce themselves as radically TBA. And queerness cannot put pleasure to use to affirm and authenticate an order that predicates politics in imaginary identities in the future. To remain 'live,' pleasure and queer must refuse the false hope of unity, the realisation of the social subject and the regulatory effects of the politics of signification.

Notes

7   This chapter is a slightly revised version of a paper I was invited to deliver as the guest keynote speaker at the Education and the Body Seminar, held in Exeter in September 2008. In the spirit of the dialogue in which I participated, I have left much of the text in the conversational style in which I presented these ideas.

8   Information on these companies' crimes comes from www.citizenworks.org and www.forbes.com. Accessed July 23, 2008. The list of GLSEN's corporate sponsors can be found at http://www.glsen.org/cgi-bin/iowa/all/donate/sponsors/index.html. Accessed July 23, 2008.

7

Bodies and minds: essentialism, activism and strategic disruptions in the primary school and beyond

Elizabeth Atkinson and Andrew Moffat

This chapter provides an alternative perspective to the queer critique offered by Cullen and by Youdell. It offers a dialogue between two members of the research team regarding the risks and rewards of presenting lesbian- and gay-identified selves within and beyond the classroom. The authors explore their own histories and practices in a dialogue constructed from excerpts from web-based discussions and interviews, and examine the discourses underpinning their own narratives. Following Nixon's examination of safe, troubled and dangerous spaces, the chapter explores how these are generated through particular performances of self, and what other possibilities might be foreclosed by these performances.

Introduction

In this chapter, we explore the significance of the introduction of our own gay bodies into educational spaces, and their potential to unsettle norms around permissible, legible identities in school contexts. As Deborah Youdell (2006a) observed, the presence of 'impossible bodies' in educational spaces can disrupt dominant discourses, and as DePalma and Atkinson pointed out in the opening chapter of this book, making some of these impossible bodies visible can forge new echochains of connotation which, while always vulnerable to recuperation by heteronormative discourses, open up possibilities for performative resignification of wounded (gay) identities.

We illustrate how, in our own experience as project team members who identify as gay and lesbian, the discourses of essentialism and gay rights have often taken strategic precedence over the more fluid discourses of queer. For both Elizabeth, as the project director, and Andy, as a teacher researcher, there have been many occasions when the need to assert and affirm a gay rights discourse has seemed paramount, whether in the classroom or in the broader policy and media arenas. Yet we have both been aware of the alternative understandings and disruptions that might be foreclosed by the stances we have taken, and debate over these issues has formed a key focus for discussions across the project team.

Each of us has experienced a conceptual shift during the course of the project in relation to the deliberate deployment of gay identities. For Elizabeth, the shift has been from theory to praxis: it was strategically important for her from the beginning to name heteronormativity, and later gender normativity, as dominant discourses to be challenged through the affirmation of LGBT identities. But at the same time, she was coming from a feminist post-structuralist perspective which refused the seeming certainties of contemporary pedagogical discourse and aimed to trouble these certainties through an undoing of boundaries and binaries around identities, research and practice. For Andy, the shift has been in the opposite direction: starting with an urgent need to assert and affirm a positive gay identity, the ways in which this might encompass an affirmation of fluidity rather than a fixing of categories have come increasingly sharply into focus. While the need to affirm the legitimacy of non-heterosexual identities has remained paramount for him, the ways in which these identities are expressed and explored have become more open to negotiation.

While strategic essentialism has played a key part in our performances of self during the course of the project, we have been aware of the tendency tone down our – or others' – gay identities to make them safe for public consumption. As Smith points out:

> There is a distinction ... between homosexuality as subversive difference, which disrupts the social order, and homosexuality as accidental difference which can be added to the social order without any fundamental transformation ... The law-abiding and not-diseased subject who keeps her expression of difference strictly behind closed doors in a monogamous relation-

ship with another adult, the 'good homosexual', is distinguished from the publicly flaunting element which strives to reproduce itself by seducing the innocent young. This element could be called the dangerous queer. (1994:204)

However, as individuals whose lives, however safely portrayed, position us outside sexual norms and expectations, we are drawn to what Susan Birden describes as an 'Out-Siders' praxis,' following Virginia Woolf's notion of 'Out-Siders' as 'those who side with the out' (2005:22). Birden states, 'Praxis, in its simplest construal, means 'theory plus action" (*ibid*). It is perhaps in this crucial juxtaposition of theory and action that the need for strategic essentialism may be the deepest. It is what allows the translation of a radical uncertainty into a practical possibility, a place where 'not knowing' (Lather, 1993) becomes a starting-point from which to act. As Caputo reminds us, 'deconstruction offers us no excuse not to act' (1993:4), but we ask ourselves here what the motivations, benefits and risks are of actions which present legible/intelligible identities. As Judith Butler asks, 'Can the visibility of identity *suffice* as a political strategy, or can it only be the starting point for a strategic inter- vention which calls for a transformation of policy?' (1991:19).

Speaking the unspeakable through activist and queer discourses

Much of the project's work (see, for example Chapter 5, and Atkinson and DePalma, 2008b) has been about speaking the unspeakable and making possible the impossible in forbidden places. But while for some this has meant affirmation through LGBT activism, drawing on liberal pluralist and strategic essentialist discourses (Atkinson, 2008), for others the desired unspeakable and impossible are further out of reach, more nebulous and less prone to fixing yet another set of legible identi- ties than liberal pluralism would allow. From this perspective liberal pluralism and its attendant affirmation of a rights discourse is seen to shore up the norm through the acceptance or tolerance of the margins, and to prevent the exploration of other more radical starting points for queering the classroom. While one perspective (Colley, 2003) is that to name a discourse is to take the first step in challenging it, another is that the very naming is to fix it in place. Ironically, working within queer theory brings up both these perspectives. As Atkinson and DePalma

97

(2009) have pointed out elsewhere, the naming of the heterosexual matrix – one of the pillars of queer theory – brings with it the danger that it becomes part of the mechanism of its own maintenance. A crucial question becomes whether refusing or 'unbelieving' the constraints and constructions of the matrix might enable us to see other possibilities and other readings for performances of self.

In this chapter we offer a series of snapshots which illustrate these performances of self in a variety of contexts and examine the discourses which have shaped them. These extracts are drawn from discussions and transcripts on the research team's private web forum, which serves simultaneously as a site of data collection and data analysis (and where these discussions themselves constitute both) and analytical emails between project team members. They include extracts from email and web-based conversations between Andy and Elizabeth and extracts from transcripts of recorded conversations between Andy and Fin Cullen, our London and Midlands regional researcher, whose conversations with each of us have repeatedly challenged our thinking and positioning, plus extracts from our contributions to broader web discussions across the whole research team. Recombined to create a new dialogue, these snapshots demonstrate the discursive processes at play which shape how we conceptualise, represent and interpret the project. We present them here with brief interpretive comments (in italics) and close the chapter with a summary of the discourses which have shaped our positions and our exchanges.

Playing with fire: safe spaces; dangerous spaces
Elizabeth
As a lesbian researcher setting out to explore sexualities equality five or six years ago, I was a) warned by colleagues to keep my politics separate from my professional life; b) advised to stick to something safer, like race (!); and c) discouraged from openly naming myself as a supporting staff member for gay and lesbian student teachers on our primary training courses.

Andy
I'd talked to my head teacher for two years about coming out at school because I'd done all this work ... all very pastoral ... you know at lunchtime we'd talk about ourselves, about what we do ... lots of circle time

things, emotional literacy stuff, how do you feel ... So all my work is about that and yet I felt I wasn't being honest to the children. And several times I was getting them to be open and honest to me and yet the biggest thing about me I was keeping a secret ... I really resented that. I wanted so badly to come out ... basically it all happened because I had my civil partnership. And I just started to think if I was straight and getting married it would be nice in the assembly, there would be a big thing, the children would know about it and make me cards. I am getting married for God's sake, why am I not telling the children, this is ridiculous.

For each of us, the desire to be identified and identifiable as gay/lesbian was both a driving need and a lurking fear: the attempts by Elizabeth's colleagues to divert and/or silence her and to draw a line between the personal and professional and the two years of conversations between Andy and his head teacher before he finally came out at school illustrate the perceived elision between being openly gay/lesbian and being simultaneously perceived as both dangerous and in danger.

Andy

I did it in circle time, just within a kind of game. It was a truth and lie game and we all said two lies and one truth and can you guess what the lies and what the truth is. And I ... I've got four sisters, I was born in Australia and I am getting married at the weekend. And someone said 'Oh, you are getting married?' and I said 'Yes, to my partner David'. Right, your turn and we carried on. And that was at half past two and by quarter past three literally the whole of the school was talking about it. Have you heard that Mr Moffat is gay, he is getting married, he is getting married to a man. But I talked to the teachers beforehand and I said 'Look I am going to do this. If any kids ask you I want you to say yes, isn't that brilliant, I am going to the wedding, it's wonderful, isn't it' ... And then no kids came up to me but every teacher had kids coming up to them to say 'Is it true Mr Moffat is gay?' and 'Is it true that Mr Moffat is getting married to a man?' ... [Recently] one of the mums [at school] talked about her son who was in the Y6 class when I first came out two years ago. She said her son came home and said 'Mr Moffat's gay' and she didn't know what to say so she said 'Mr Moffat's happy, you mean', to which her son replied 'he is happy, and he's got a boyfriend too!'

The normalisation of same-sex relationships through the recognition of the socially acceptable practice of legally endorsed, committed mono-gamy (albeit under the othering label of civil partnership rather than marriage) is juxtaposed here with the disruption of the norm through the image of the impossible body (clearly a source of astonishment for the pupils at Andy's school) – a man's male spouse at a wedding ceremony. As discussed in Chapter 1, the recognition and performance of legal partnerships for same-sex couples can be read as both profoundly queer in its disruption of the patriarchal and oppressive connotations of mar-riage and profoundly normative in its acquiescence with the upholding of hierarchies of acceptable and unacceptable relationship patterns. For both of us, the act of marrying our same-sex partners has been a (poten-tially queer) repudiation of heteronormativity and also a statement of gay pride, while for others such an act represents nothing more than the reinforcement (or perhaps minimal expansion) of the status quo.

Being a role model: a two-edged sword?

Andy

See for me I have a massive thing about role models because I felt that I didn't have any when I grew up. You know, I want to be a good gay, a good role model for any gay child who is growing up ... I did have girl-friends when I was little but you know, I am so conscious of portraying this image of a gay man, thinking oh God, I don't want to ... It's almost as if I want to say no, I had boyfriends actually [laughs]. I know, I know, it's ridiculous ... completely ridiculous. But there was this whole thing about not wanting to confuse them, wanting them to be very clear, look I am gay therefore I like men, you know ... [I was saying recently to Fin that] I am still thinking I should cut my hair ... I went into a year six class. They were appalling, they were really badly behaved. And as I walked in they were all tittering. And I know it's because of my hair. There is no other reason why they'd titter. Fin said she's worked with quite a few male teachers and youth workers with long hair. I said, 'Is it high-lighted?' She said, 'A lot of them are blond. I don't think it's highlighted.' And I said, 'Yeah, you see.'

Elizabeth

I can 'pass' as straight – and frequently do – and sometimes use this to make myself seem less threatening to anxious head teachers or nosy reporters – and I notice that, while I am completely out in my academic and university lecturing life, I avoid telling members of the press that I am a lesbian, for fear that they will somehow feel that this negates the value of the whole *No Outsiders* project. So what does that say about the right of LGBT people to research the area of their own sexual identity? Is this research LESS legitimate because it's headed up by a lesbian?

Andy's desire to present a fictionalised version of himself as having had boyfriends when he was younger and Elizabeth's heterosexual or lesbian performance of self according to context illustrate the hierarchy of acceptability of sexual identities: it is better/safer to appear straight than gay and better/safer to appear gay than bi. And bi is an identity marker that neither of us has chosen to claim (see 'The absent B and T' below for further discussion), preferring instead the safer trappings of respectable gayness. And we both make conscious choices about the deployment of symbols of gayness in our performances of self, being aware, yet again, of the sense of being both dangerous and in danger when we choose to use these symbols to make ourselves intelligibly gay. The danger here, of course, is not only of limiting the repertoire of recognised symbols of gayness for ourselves and others, but of failing to recognise that these symbols (such as long, highlighted blonde hair for a man) may have other or no meanings in different contexts, and that countless people who identify as gay may not choose to use them, or may be unaware of them. Furthermore, in Elizabeth's discussion of passing, there is also the sense that one needs to do nothing to pass as straight other than choose not to deploy gay-identified symbols and discourses: an assumption that reinforces the concept of heterosexuality as the norm rather than as also being performatively and discursively constructed.

The dangerous homosexual

Andy

There was one time I wrote [on the project web forum] about: the discussion was about the whole gay penguin thing and are we just presenting images of gays being in happy families. And I said something like look, we do need to talk about gay people being in happy families because there isn't any representation of that. We don't need to talk about gay saunas and cottaging, I didn't say that but something like that, something that was still up there at a later date and then I started worrying, I was worried about I hope that people don't think that I am saying that's what gay life is about, gay saunas and ... I can't remember what it was, something else. Something seedy. [Looking back, what I actually said was] I think at this point in the children's lives we should be promoting safe images of gay people and gay families, to redress the balance. We need to talk about gay people falling in love because that image has been hidden for so long. They can find out about saunas and gaydar when they come out in their teens!

Again, the spectre of the dangerous homosexual rears its head – this time in an explicit call for safe representations of gay people and gay families. As Nixon has pointed out (see Chapter 4), the absolute requirement to maintain the impression that educators – and especially teachers of young children – follow only one pattern of sexual activity belies the varied reality of both heterosexual and non-heterosexual teachers' (and others') lives. A similar fear of bringing contamination into childhood purity was expressed by Elizabeth after visiting another project school to do some literacy and art work with 5 to 6 year-old children, based on the same story of gay penguins mentioned above by Andy (Parnell et al, 2005):

I noticed myself *not* taking photos of the less artistically mature pictures – eg C's and B's – first because they were less obviously penguins (or that's what I told myself) but then, underlying this, because I imagined the newspapers saying 'Look at how they are getting hold of children who aren't even old enough to draw or paint properly and brainwashing them' ... And I did the same with the writing – avoiding taking photos of the children's tiny hands doing the writing because it made them seem so innocent; hesitating before photographing anything that might seem as though they'd been indoctrinated into PC gay-loving-ness. (And all this, still in the absolute conviction that this project is doing the right thing!)

Here the hetero-norm is put to work to maintain social stability, and when we feel ourselves threatening it, we fear we are rocking the founda-tions of our world. In such a context, pursuing a gay essentialist strategy is itself a strategic disruption; but it is one which is always open, as in this case, to recuperation.

Pushing boundaries and being (or not being) a rebel

Andy

I don't joke with straight men, 'Oh, phwoar, he's nice' but you know, I always joke with women. Every day with the women, female teachers or staff or the dinner ladies, it will be, 'Oh, look Andy, there's a postman outside' or a fireman, you know, but I won't do that with the straight men ... I made my gayness acceptable by laughing about it with people ... I am making it safe ... by laughing about it ... this is why I worry about the whole camp thing and about wearing a holly outfit in the Christmas [pantomime], I am just perpetuating the whole John Ingram[9] thing. I am not pushing boundaries at all, not changing their ideas. I worry that I am doing myself and the gay cause, you know, the gay sort of agenda a disservice ... Am I just perpetuating the whole idea of what a gay man is? ... It wasn't so bad last year because actually I was being very straight ... you know, we were all sailors wearing white tight t-shirts and hats, but this year I've got a holly bush on and I am dancing around faldilala, now that's big fairy, that's like a big gay thing.

Notwithstanding Andy's interesting illustration of straightness by recourse to the established camp image of sailors in white tight t-shirts, the concern over the perpetuation of gay stereotypes illustrates the tensions between acting as a role model and disrupting norms. As Andy illustrates, he is making his gayness safe by laughing about it. In sharing his laughter with women but not with men, he is perhaps also perpetuating the hierarchy that privileges heteromasculinity over all other forms of sexuality and gender expression. To laugh with the women is to show allegiance with them as lesser human beings; to exaggerate campness (and its association with perceptions of femininity) is to emphasise the division between gay men (and heterosexual women) and real men.

Elizabeth

I've *always* been torn between 'being good' and 'being a rebel' – whether it was teaching reading in my Reception class in my NQT [newly qualified teacher] year, where I refused to use reading schemes and got into trouble with the head ... to jumping through Standards hoops with students while not believing in the whole crazy system which they uphold ... So what's different? I think what's different is that, before, all the 'safe' things were the things I was rebelling against – reading schemes, National Literacy Strategy, 'Standards' criteria etc. – but now, the 'safe' thing is at the same time the 'dangerous' thing, because however safe it is, some people still won't even go near it. So I have to play safe in order to play dangerously – but at the same time, there's always the risk that I'll slip into the safeness myself – which I was beginning to do – instead of keeping the critical edge. And ... there is a danger that ... the whole project might slip that way and become dangerously depoliticised – which is also why I'm becoming deeply interested in how the project is rekindling dormant activisms in a lot of its participants ...

The question of what makes pedagogy – and other forms of practice – safe and unsafe takes on a new dimension here: perhaps Elizabeth's earlier disruptions and refusals in the areas of literacy teaching and the assessment of teacher training were, in some ways, queerer than her liberal pluralist/gay rights activist incursions into the unsafe territory of heterogender normativity. Yet as Nixon has illustrated in Chapter 4 in relation to the moral panic in the media over the project's work, the fact that the safest acts – reading a story, talking about families – become unsafe in the context of the project's work also gives them the potential to disrupt norms through the shifting of the ground on which safeness and norms rest, in addition to the potential simply to reinforce that ground by the reiteration of otherness. So we are perhaps remaking and stabilising the ground at one and the same time.

Histories and identities: our pasts and our presents
Elizabeth

What does it say about the private/public, personal/professional divide – if there is one – when I find myself sitting in the Cathedral of the city where I went to school, watching Sue's school parade their rainbow banner down the aisle? This is where we went to respectable concerts, for heaven's sake! This Cathedral Green (oh yes, it has to have capitals) is where we used to meet up with other schools for country dancing festivals. This small city is where I had my first experiences of (heterosexual) romance, and where I was amorously pursued when I was 13 and 14 by a much-hated and marginalised young lesbian, whom I tried to cure with Christianity ... This is the small city where my best friend and I (I'll call her Belinda – she was a policeman's daughter, which always seems significant) rolled naked on the hay bales in a shed near her house, pretending to be a grown-up man and woman, and played 'doctors' in my bedroom, never once connecting our explorations of each other's bodies with love, sexual attraction or lesbian relationships.

The recuperation of the hetero-norm is deeply embedded in Elizabeth's narrative. Heterosexual romance (with the heterosexual merely added in parenthesis, as this is of course what romance means) is implicitly opposed to homosexual predation and the acts of sexual pretence carried out by two young girls are seen as natural practice for adult heterosexual coupling. Furthermore, all the trappings of the establishment – Church, State (and its instrument the school) and folk tradition – are paraded as significations not of the constraints of the heterosexual matrix but simply of the ordinary life that we all lead. At the same time these significations are recruited to the matrix as unshakeable monoliths against which the tiny fist of a lesbian presence will almost certainly batter to no avail. Leaving aside for a moment the assumptions underlying the universalisation of country dancing and concerts in the cathedral as every child's lived experience, the message here is that by simply entering the environment in which these innocent childhood pursuits had taken place as a lesbian adult, Elizabeth comprised a sort of automatic contamination, with the added implication that the only way to infiltrate normality with such a dangerous presence is to do it well away from home.

Andy

I moved away from [my home town] when I was 18 and although I now live there again it's the other side of the city to my parents and it takes half an hour to visit them. Whenever I drive over there, to the place I grew up, I feel uncomfortable. The place makes me feel angry. Similarly as I drive away there is a sense of relief. I know this is because the place reminds me of being closeted as a teenager and feeling desperately unhappy. Walking around the small town centre reminds me of the feeling that I was isolated, and that there was no way out. There is a lot of anger in me towards that place. I thought going back there with my partner would change the way it made me feel, but it didn't. It just made me feel insecure.

Andy still feels the constraints of the heterosexual matrix almost as a physical presence in his home town: the experience of being isolated in the crowd and trapped both by the closet and by the demands of hetero-normativity provides Andy with ample motivation for the presentation of gay identity which has become a central part of his personal and professional life. And as the following extract demonstrates, the matrix made itself felt from the early years of Andy's childhood experience.

Andy

When I was in school, when I was about 8, I won a competition in school and I sang 'A little peace' by Nicole, Germany's winning Eurovision song ... And I wore a dress and a floppy hat, to be her, to perform. And I won the competition. And looking back I realise now that it was the first time I used drama. The first time I realised I am actually good at something, I can use drama to make children laugh. Lots of children were going oh, that was great, that was great, that was great. And you know in those days if you weren't good at sport as a boy you had no status at all. So it was the first time I thought I was popular and it was because I wore a dress and sang a song. So I spoiled it basically by ... wearing the dress to go home. And I think I did it because I wanted to retain that popularity but outside the stage ... It made me feel good. I felt good wearing a dress. So I wore a dress going home and got beaten up ... But there is not a picture of [me being Nicole] at all. For me that was the proudest moment of my childhood, you know, I will always remember that. And I wish that somebody had taken a photo of me in that dress and that guitar. But no, why isn't there a picture of me in that dress with the guitar? ... there are a couple of me playing football ... God knows how they could have possibly found me playing ... There's me and my bike. It's as you would expect, you know.

The surplus visibility Andy experienced – and its disturbingly violent consequence – by the simple act of wearing a dress outside the sanctioned arena of 'performance' contrasts ironically with the invisibility through which the wearing of the dress is erased by its absence from representations of himself as a child. And the absence of the dress – and of Andy's desired performance of self – is all the more marked because of the presence of the heteronormal – the football and the bike. So Andy's childhood is shaped through both presence and absence, with visibility and invisibility working together to reinforce the norm and to erase the abnormal, while his desire to reassert the visible reappears in his adult life.

The absent 'B' and 'T': bi and trans identities

Elizabeth

My own personal history around gender identity seemed at first un-problematic. While I have deliberately, consistently challenged trainee primary teachers, for example, to justify their assumption that I am a woman, and shocked them by emphasising that I may not always have been one, my sense of gendered identity remained unrocked until a) I fell in love with a woman – when for a brief moment I wondered, foolishly, whether this somehow made me in some way into a man – and b) some fifteen years later, I attended a transgender conference where we were all invited to write our preferred personal pronoun along with our preferred name onto our badges. 'It's only the trans people here who need to do that,' I found myself thinking. 'Everyone can tell from my name and my appearance that I'm a proper woman.' (!)

As a whole team, perhaps our queerest moments, in terms of encounters with and challenges to our unspoken assumptions, have been in our explorations of gender expression and gender identity, led and supported by Jay Stewart of Gendered Intelligence (www.genderedintelligence.org. uk). The naïveté of Elizabeth's response to the challenges of a trans-friendly environment, and of her fear that her love for a woman must make her a man, both speak of the elision of sex-gender-sexuality within the heterosexual/heterogender matrix and demonstrate the queering and subversion of gender norms presented by the spectrum of trans identities.

Andy

I haven't even thought about [transgender stuff], to be fair. And I wouldn't know where to start. I am taking it one step at a time. Let's just deal with gay and lesbian things. Even bisexual, I mean, really, you know, it's hard, it's hard. Because what I am saying to people, what I am sort of preaching in my lesson plan to people is that you don't choose to be gay. It's like having blue eyes or red hair, you know, you are gay or you are not gay. But bisexual fucks all that up. So actually can you not be bi-sexual, please. [laughs] ... because on the one hand you want to say look, we have *No Outsiders*, it's equality, you can love who you want to love like I was saying to the kids. But then that's like saying you've got a choice. You haven't got a choice. If you are gay, you are gay. It's not like, you know, I might want to love a woman but I can't. I love men. So it does make things very complicated that does, it ruins my whole scheme quite frankly [laughs] ... let's deal with [the more complex issues] when we are all talking about gay people existing. At the moment gay people don't exist in the primary curriculum, you know, and in schools.

Elizabeth

I suppose one of the things about bi identities – whether or not they have that term attached to them (I hate the idea that people might describe me as bi) is that they carry within them the promise of impermanence – how can you have one lifelong partner if you're attracted to both sexes? So bi seems inherently more dangerous, perhaps, than straight or gay – and of course, you can never trust bi people – you never know which way they'll turn ... How can we overcome all this guff and present the notion of being attracted to, and happy to love, both sexes as being just as stable as any other identity? . . What do we teach children when they first enter pre-school educational settings (whether the 'formal' setting of the nursery or the 'informal' playgroup)? Sorting and matching! What goes with what; what belongs in what category; what doesn't belong. Oh yes, we have interlocking/overlapping circles when we do venn diagrams showing how some things can belong to more than one category – but do we do this about gender? Or sexuality? Not yet! Or do we ask whether and why we need gender or sexuality categories? Not yet!

Neither of us has ever presented as bi, and while a number of members of the project team have had relationships with people of both genders, none have chosen identify openly as bi within the context of the project. For many people, the need to erase heterosexual pasts is part of the motivation to assert a homosexual present, which becomes all too difficult if bi enters the picture. If gay is dangerous, then bi as constituted by the discourses of heteronormativity is clearly more dangerous still: what worse threat than that of the predatory homosexual, after all, than the threat of the undercover agent who could equally well turn their pre-dation in either direction, or could abandon the permanence of a relationship with one gender for the lure of a relationship with the other? The message that comes across clearly here is the perceived imper-manence of bisexuality as a component within a relationship – which contrasts oddly and illogically with the known and recognised imper-manence of many heterosexual bondings – and the assumed superiority of long-term commitment to one partner over long-term or short-term relationships to multiple partners – whether simultaneous or serial.

Concluding reflections

The processes underlying our performances of self in the examples presented here are illustrated by the primacy of categorisation and labelling in our discussions; the difficulty of introducing a queer perspective once these categories have become situated as the frame for our discourse; the (consciously and subconsciously) felt need to maintain the image of the safe homosexual; and the tensions between achieving tangible effects in children's and colleagues' thinking and behaviour, and working towards a more disruptive, de-normalising queer practice. The exposure of these discourses raises questions about the implications of presenting ourselves as uncomplicatedly and safely gay; the normalisation of stable, romantic gay relationships and the hierarchisation of such relationships over other relationship patterns; the privileging of gay/lesbian over bisexual identity; the taken-for-granted elision, albeit within a homonormative, rather than heteronormative matrix, of sex-gender-sexuality in our performances of self; and the concomitant erasure of transgender and/or gender-queer possibilities. They also demonstrate the need for us to disavow heterosexual experience in our own lives for fear that it might contaminate the legitimacy of our present gay selves.

Conversely, the examples we have presented illustrate the role and value of a strategic essentialism, drawing on liberal humanist and social justice perspectives, in presenting legible gay selves in a world where simply to claim or affirm a non-normative identity may, in a sense, be queer enough. They also illustrate the personal and emotional value of claiming such non-normative identities for ourselves as teachers, parents and/or children.

We offer these presentations of self as illuminative of our experience within and beyond the *No Outsiders* project. The questions they raise are pertinent to our own thinking, to the debate within the project and to wider debates within the educational and social world. There is no right way to do this work, or to be ourselves. But the different ways in which we and others have approached the interrogation and disruption of heteronormativity offer starting points, we hope, for further consideration of how to do, be and think the differences that may make a difference to all of us.

Note

9   The late John Ingram's highly camp character, Mr Humphreys, with his catch line, 'I'm free', not only became the hallmark of the popular British department store sitcom, 'Are you being served?' (1972 to 1985) but continued a trend of two-dimensional camp portrayals in film and television which virtually obliterated other representations of gay identity.

8

A democratic community of practice: Unpicking all those words

Renée DePalma and Laura Teague

One of the questions which occupied the project team from the outset was the possibility of creating and maintaining a democratic process for the team-members within the operation of the project itself: a project which brought with it the continuing possibility of the mobilisation of hierarchies of power on a number of fronts. In this chapter DePalma and Teague analyse of the complex, uncertain and sometimes painful process of building an intentional research community that involves people from very different practice communities (primary schools and universities). As members of these two different communities (the senior researcher and a teacher researcher), the authors reflect on this process of building and maintaining such a community, particularly focusing on attempts to foster democratic relationships among participants.

> It does not matter that I did not mean – consciously, at any rate – to take power; what matters is what got meant. (Moje, 2000:34).

In the original funding proposal, the *No Outsiders* research consortium was defined as a global action research community (Somekh, 2005), drawing, as Somekh does, upon the Cultural Historical Activity Theory (CHAT) notion of a community of practice. While the word 'community', for some, may carry connotations of harmony and even homogeneity, the project proposal anticipated that much of the project development would emerge from *dissensus,* rather than consensus, 'What makes engagement in practice possible and productive is as much a matter of diversity as it is a matter of homogeneity' (Wenger, 1998:75).

Heterogeneity was implicit in the project design, which paired teacher researchers, as privileged and expert insiders to the teaching practice, with university-based research assistants who would provide both an outsider perspective and a particular expertise in research methodologies. The hope was to create dialogic relationships that would contest hierarchies, and the project proposal explicitly stated that fully dialogical relationships can best be achieved when 'academics' and 'practitioners' work together as co-researchers to challenge traditional hierarchies which separate the researcher from the researched. Thus data collection tools such as interviews, observations and on-line communications are recognised as complex and power-laden, and the right of the researcher to interpret the researched is not taken as automatic.

In addition, the project's shared focus on sexualities equality required us to negotiate our own understandings of what that might mean in our own particular local practices (DePalma and Atkinson, in press) and how that (re)positioned us in terms of our professional and personal identities (Allan, Hemingway, and Jennett, 2007; Atkinson, 2008; Nixon and East, 2008). This chapter explores how participants negotiated the terms by which we brought our own sexual identities into our group discussions.

From the inside, as we have been participated in the on-going process of building this community, we step back momentarily and endeavour to take this process apart, drawing upon Walkerdine's metaphor of un-picking the knitting:

> How we carry out the research, what questions we ask, what counts as data, what is judged to be true are all entangled in the pursuit of 'the truth', and we get caught up in this too. Our research becomes a process of disentangling, of pulling ourselves free of the web. It is like unpicking knitting, the wool still bearing the imprint of the knots which formed it into a garment. This garment often seemed to fit us well and even to keep us warm on winter nights. Taking it apart can be painful and does not reveal the easy certainty of answers. (1998:15)

Analysing the web-based and email discussions that participants had over the course of the first year of the *No Ousiders* project, we specifically focus on the early negotiations of the hierarchical relationships among teacher researchers and university researchers. These discussions were permeated with themes of data ownership and surveillance, the effect of academic discourse, the different goals and constraints of practitioners and academics and the nature and status of research and practice. Specifically drawing upon these themes, we analyse the assumptions about *community, practice* and *democracy* that underpin our intentionally designed democratic community of practice by examining our own negotiations of power, trust and ownership during the first year of the project. Rather than providing guidelines for establishing and maintaining a democratic community of practice, we examine the complexities inherent in the process. We argue that the negotiation process itself is a crucial aspect of collaboration and recommend resisting the temptation to expect these negotiations to minimise dissent and reach compromise.

A community of practice as a vehicle for a participatory action research (PAR) project

The community of practice model (Lave and Wenger, 1991; Wenger, 1998) was adopted for the *No Outsiders* project because it seems particularly attuned to the processes and assumptions underpinning participatory action research (PAR). Underpinning the notion of communities of practice is Lave's understanding that learning is not separated from the practice itself, 'Learning is an integral aspect of activity in and with the world at all times' (1996:8). In their description of communities of practice, Lave and Wenger invoke what they refer to as a long Marxist tradition of rejecting mind-body dualisms to emphasise 'relational interdependency of agent and world, activity, meaning, cognition, learning, and knowing' (1991:50). This resonates with the fundamental tradition in action research that rejects the separation of research and practice:

> Action research is simply a form of self-reflective enquiry undertaken by participants in social situations in order to improve the rationality and justice of their own practices, their understanding of these practices, and the situations in which the practices are carried out. (Carr and Kemmis, 1986:162)

The fusing of participant-learner positions characterises the purposeful process of expansive learning in which 'the motivation for learning is an increase in the power-to-act in the real world, characterised by an increase in the actions available to the individual' (Roth *et al*, 2000).

German psychologist Kurt Lewin is generally credited with coining the term 'action research' and is widely considered the 'father' of action research, but since Lewin's work in the 1940s, action research has evolved into a complex array of approaches with different underlying philosophies and concerns (Kemmis, 1993; Westlander, 2006). While Lewin's original notion of action research was relatively researcher-driven, there has been an increasing trend toward more collaborative ventures where fundamental aspects of the research are constantly negotiated by practitioner and professional researcher in a version coined by William Foote Whyte (1991) as participatory action research (PAR). The community of practice and PAR frameworks were explicitly linked in the original *No Outsiders* project proposal as a way to challenge hierarchical relations between research and practice, researcher and researched, and the proposal included a plan to conduct an ongoing meta-investigation of these processes alongside the particular projects taking place in school sites throughout the UK:

> The study is based on an ecological perspective, which strongly implicates the researcher as an inseparable part of the reality studied. This requires not only an explicit description of the researcher's participation in the classroom, but also an explicit analysis of how the researcher's thoughts changed as a result of participation (Carson and Sumara, 1997). To this end, we plan to collect and analyse existing data (focused discussion transcripts, web discussion postings, research assistant reports, and our own communication) to explore the potential of a research-based community of practice to create spaces for professional development. In this sense, we will be conducting our own action research project along with the teacher researchers. (excerpt from *No Outsiders* research proposal, *Case for Support*)

As mentioned earlier, the project designers were particularly interested in the process of community building through negotiation and dissensus, particularly since teacher researchers were expected to generate the goals and objectives of their action research projects based on their classroom experience and concerns, while research assistants were expected to take the role of research consultants and 'critical friends' (Campbell *et al*, 2004:106). They had no idea what the research projects would look like or what kinds of relationships might emerge among the

No Outsiders community members. They embraced PAR knowing that negotiations among different parties, with different understandings of ethics, goals and interests, reinvents each PAR project as unique, 'the course of events is to a great extent unpredictable, offers unexpected twists and turns, and ... initial overall research planning is not possible to follow without striking out new paths' (Westlander, 2006:60). This unpredictability was both exhilarating and terrifying, and offered an opportunity to 'explore an ecological approach to ethics through continual negotiation of power, language and authentic participation that is particularly compatible with the participatory nature of collaborative action research' (Collins, 2004:349).

Whose community? Whose practice?

Nel Noddings reminds us that 'Community is not an unalloyed good; it has a dark side' (1996:245), illustrating her point by demonstrating that both Nazi sympathisers and non-Jews who rescued Jews during the Holocaust attributed their actions to the values of their respective communities. The word 'community' can be misleading because popular usage leads us to believe that we think we know what it means. We tend to take the word to imply an unproblematic, normative group failing to consider implicit potential for (even inevitability of) power dynamics and conflicts, 'the reification of community in ordinary forms of language can lead us to neglect the messy relations between individuals and communities' (Linehan and McCarthy, 2001:130). Lave and Wenger are careful to qualify their notion of community to incorporate diversity:

> In using the term community, we do not imply some primordial culture-sharing entity. We assume that members have different interests, make diverse contributions to activity, and hold varied viewpoints ... Nor does the term community imply necessarily co-presence, a well-defined identifiable group, or socially visible boundaries. It does imply participation in an activity system about which participants share understandings concerning what they are doing and what that means in their lives and for their communities. (1991:97-98)

Drawing upon Bakhtin's (1999) notion of heteroglossia, Winkelmann notes that community is inhabited by multiple and conflicting voices and argues that by turning community into a simplified, stable commodity 'we ignore the tension inherent in the very dynamics of language and the dynamism demanded of the continuous action and reflection, action and reflection, of genuine praxis' (1991:24). It is this heteroglossia that we focus on in this analysis.

Kemmis reminds us that we cannot conceptualise research without attending to the institutional contexts within which this research takes place:

> as a social practice, [research] is always and inevitably socially- and historically-constructed. We begin to see how the social practice which is research is a social practice which relates to (and has its meaning in a context of) other social practices like those involved in serving a bureaucracy, or participating in the practices which constitute a disciplinary field, or participating in social movements. (1993)

No Outsiders might actually be seen as a hybrid research community, since members of two pre-existing institutional practice communities were intentionally brought together to transform the way each institution operated separately (the way academics researched and the way teachers taught). The reality was in fact much more complex, as each individual simultaneously participated in various communities of practice (Rock, 2005; Wenger, 1998) and action research in particular provides 'different imperatives, different affordances and different meanings for participants depending on their positioning within overlapping, inter-related communities of practice' (Somekh, 2006).

In *No Outsiders*, people were positioned not only in terms of their relationship within the community (university researcher – teacher researcher, South West group — London group) but also in terms of their positions in their regular (long-term) practice communities. University researchers include those with a broad range of experience and institutional status, from graduate students finishing PhD theses to established researchers. Some were relatively new to sexualities research; others were unfamiliar with action research. Primary school-based participants were similarly diverse in terms of their own institutional positioning, from the head teacher of a tiny rural Church school to a first-year teacher in a diverse urban school, for example. In this analysis we will focus on the ways in which simultaneous participation in either the (primary) school community or academic research community affected *No Outsiders* participants' engagement with the 'joint enterprise' (Wenger, 1998) of addressing (LGBT) equalities in primary schools.

The project started in September 2006 with a national meeting of all project participants. Aside from one other national meeting (January 2007) and an additional regional meeting in each of the three regions, most group communication during the first year of the project took place by e-mail or via the project website, which included a password-protected asynchronous discussion forum for project members. In early October, in response to some email reflections on power and democracy within the project that she received from Laura (teacher researcher and co-author of this chapter), Elizabeth, the principal investigator, initiated a new discussion to the *No Outsiders* web forum entitled 'Is our project democratic?':

> I'd really like to start a discussion about this, as it's absolutely central to how the project develops – but I'd very much like it to be in a separate discussion on the left hand menu, because that way it will always stay visible for us to come back to and rethink ... as Laura, one of our teacher researchers, has already pointed out in a very thoughtful and thought-provoking email, we still know who holds the power, and who is interpreting whom! Yet in this very statement, she turns the tables, and quite rightly starts interpreting the actions of the university-based research team.

This posting led to a discussion about the possible ways in which the affordances and constraints of our institutional communities, as well as certain cultural understandings of the hierarchical relationships between these two communities, affected our participation in *No Outsiders*. Some of these included:

Time to participate in discussions

Different institutional communities prioritised differently the amount of time participants were expected to devote to these negotiations. The project was designed (by two academics!) with the understanding that this kind of negotiation would be an integral part of the research. Our interactive project website was meant to facilitate the communication among physically-dispersed community members and provide a maximum flexibility in terms of space and time that would afford participation for everyone.

Nevertheless, Laura brought up early on that as a teacher she felt she would benefit from 'more explicit discussion between teacher researchers and university researchers about where this project is coming from theoretically – which is all a bit impossible because of time constraints on the teachers'. Teacher researchers did participate on the web and participation did increase somewhat over the course of the project, but particularly in the beginning the university researchers were a stronger presence. What the designers didn't anticipate was an institutional time constraint influenced by institutional definitions of legitimate practice. The project funding provided for teachers to be released from teaching obligations for a certain amount of research time, but schools were not always able to release teachers even to meet with the university researchers or attend project events, much less to spend their valuable working time on web discussions. For the university researchers, discussion and reflection was congruent with institutional practices (research and publications), while for teacher researchers discussions were typically associated with free time activities. As university researcher Elizabeth B. pointed out: 'University researchers are paid to spend time discussing research issues, teacher researchers are paid to spend time in the classroom, and must find additional time to engage with the website'.

Conflicting institutional messages

All teachers participating in *No Outsiders* had to secure permission from the head teacher (if they were not themselves the head). But this formal consent did not automatically translate into a great deal of institutional support. Even when the teacher was the head teacher, each school had a different set of negotiations to undertake with the local school community – colleagues and parents – as preparation for sexualities work that might be perceived as dangerously subversive. Different local contexts contributed to a wide discrepancy between some teachers who designed and implemented rather concrete and successful projects early on and those who, at the end of the first year, were still negotiating terms for beginning their *No Outsiders* work – for example, revising policy documents or discussing project books with peers.

Nevertheless, as members of the *No Outsiders* team, teachers were also aware of the expectation that they would produce some kind of action research project. There was a good deal of discussion about this, with university researchers insisting that those teachers who reflected on the process, even when no concrete progress was made, were also doing valuable action research. Yet some teachers seemed to feel caught between conflicting institutional demands, with the *No Outsiders* community calling for progress and schools calling for caution. Laura, for example, lamented that she felt compelled to 'do' something by the *No Outsiders* community, but was not yet ready in her teaching community, 'I'm good at thinking ... but doing is more tricky. There's no point me being involved in this if all I will do is think...'

Unequal institutional status

It was Laura who from the beginning questioned the ability of individuals to divest themselves of the power invested in them by their institutional status:

> I love the fact that this project involves teachers and head teachers and [local authority] people and academics and whoever else and its commitment to there being no outsiders is important. But simply by having all these people on board and saying we're all working together is not enough – there needs, perhaps, to be dialogue about the potential difficulties in order that we can move towards something genuinely more 'equal'.

Moje (2000) and Somekh (2002), reflecting on their own experiences with university-school collaborations, both recognise that while these collaborations are inevitably imbued with the affiliatory power of the authoritative, prestigious university institution, it would be an over-simplification to ignore other ways in which power permeates and structures these relationships. Somekh (2002) reminds us that the relatively low status of education in the academy, claims about scientific and non-scientific ways of knowing and popular negative associations with the word 'academic' can contribute to more complex power relations. Moje (2000) points out that collaborative relationships are negotiated interpersonally in terms of multiple embodied affiliations, so that what one wears or eats (or doesn't) can be interpreted in terms of power-laden associations. Nevertheless, in our hybrid community, the university-school hierarchy was felt to be a particular challenge to pro-

119

moting cross-institutional collegial relationships. Laura explained how her perceptions stemmed from her own experiences as a university student, and related these to similar teacher-pupil hierarchies she participates in within her own school:

> When I was an undergraduate I was genuinely scared of going to talk to half the lecturers. And I guess I agree that there isn't really a solution – because the imbalance of power between different groups is ingrained in society. But we can keep working towards an ideal in the way we behave towards each other ... I guess I am always in a position of power as the teacher in my classroom but I can choose how to use that power and I can do everything I can to listen to the children in my class and to help them to engage with the learning they do and to develop their own voices.

Roth argues that communities of practice are characterised by 'unquestioned background assumptions, common sense, and mundane reason' shared by members (cited in Barab and Duffy, 2000:36). In a sense, our shared understandings included a hierarchical system of binary relations (the academy/school, theory/practice) that implicitly coloured our relationships even as we challenged these binaries.

Different discourses with unequal status

Tusting (2005) draws upon Fairclough's (2003) notion of 'semiotic order' to examine how ways in which discourse is organised in particular social fields brings global social orders to bear on local semiotic interactions. Semiotic meaning is shaped by social structure that reaches beyond the moment of interaction by actors who are 'shaped by their whole history of interactions' (Tusting, 2005:42). The social order that places the academy above teaching practice places a higher value on the discourse of academia.

Somekh writes of the ways in which power relations are construed by the different discourses of university- and school-based researchers, 'Those very terms that alienated the teachers were those that would give the project status in the eyes of the academy' (2002:96). She writes that by recognising that neither discourse was more or less extensive or exclusive than the other, participants came to realise the value of possessing multiple fluencies, 'we would direct our writing to different audiences and draw each others' work to the attention of those who otherwise would not have given it credence' (*ibid*:99). Similarly, *No Out-*

siders teachers communicated with parents, colleagues, administrators, religious leaders and the press in ways that went beyond the discursive expertise of university researchers. Yet while we might explicitly recognise the value of non-academic discourse, the fact remained that teachers frequently reported that they felt excluded by the academic discourse that university researchers habitually used in web-based conversations that were meant to be inclusive. Sue, a teacher researcher, described her reaction to encountering theoretical discourse on the web discussion forum as a strong emotional sense of inadequacy and exclusion:

> [I'm] not sure what I say makes any sense. I think you are all incredibly brainy and smart, by the way ... I really don't get it, feel terribly dim, a total outsider, want to fall asleep, but also have a dreadful urge to laugh hysterically ... Am I the only one who has that reaction?!

Laura supported Sue's position, 'As much as it fascinates me and I find the concepts and frameworks ... useful tools for thinking about things, I do also find it hard to take all the jargon seriously. And it's jargon – you're totally not dim whatsoever'. Through Laura's use of the term 'jargon' she highlights that Sue is not an intellectual but a discursive outsider. Along these lines, another teacher researcher, Andi, related her own frustration with academic discourse to her experience in the Comenius program, an international, multilingual project, 'I have just returned from the Czech Republic where the group I am working with all speak a variety of languages ... believe me we have had difficulties.' And Renée tried to unpick assumptions about academic discourse and intelligence by reminding Sue that, as an outsider to UK political and school systems, she felt overwhelmed by the very discourse Sue (as an experienced head teacher) is proficient in:

> When I first started working in the UK, I was first overwhelmed by all the acronyms I had to learn ... But it wasn't just the acronyms, it was the way things are organised, who does what and why ... You were very helpful to me in that, however, because you clarified the issue (well, you clarified why it was confusing and ambiguous, but still!) when you sent us that letter to your [local authority].

The reference is to a letter Sue wrote to her local authority concerning her analysis of government guidance for schools on approaching religion and sexuality, an issue that she introduced to the *No Outsiders* discussion forum and explained at length. Sue's analysis drew upon considerable professional expertise and the careful reading of various complex government documents, a discourse that, as Renée wrote, she found initially impenetrable. While the *No Outsiders* community did rely on knowledge and expertise that was distributed across participants, so that not all participants had the same understandings of the practice as a whole (Hutchins, 1994) and this distributed expertise included valuable discursive proficiencies (Somekh, 2002), this distribution did not imply equal status.

Not-so-mutual accountability

Wenger expects communities of practice to engage in joint endeavour, where members are mutually accountable (Wenger, 1998). In his classic description of claims processors at a company he calls Alinsu, Wenger stresses that while all processors were ultimately held accountable by managers to process claims accurately and efficiently, processors negotiated this accountability with each other in an emergent shared practice. They were accountable not only to Alinsu managers, but also to each other for 'making their work life bearable' (p81, but see DePalma, in press for an analysis of the limitations of Wenger's claims processors example). Nevertheless, the way that *No Outsiders* spanned academic and school institutions meant that our accountability was split. Our shared practice emerged as a response to two different sets of 'managers,' with very different institutional goals, standards and policies.

As mentioned earlier, schools often felt accountable to their local authorities and local communities to not rock the boat. Academics were under pressure to prove themselves as productive academics which, as Moore reminds us, is not particularly congruent with this kind of endeavour, 'Academics work within institutions that are steeped in traditions and hierarchy. There are tensions between the traditional role of an academic researcher and a person who is truly committed to community based participatory research' (2004:157). Those of us who secured institutional funding for the project had an additional accountability: as project designers, Elizabeth and Renée were expected to produce something like what the ESRC had paid for. Failure to do so might seriously jeopardise their future institutional standing.

Laura pointed out that this unevenly distributed accountability further contributed to hierarchical relations, 'I guess to move further towards there being more equality between university researchers and teacher researchers ... teacher researchers [would have] to have been (and be) more involved in decisions about the project.'

Shifting notions of democracy

These discussions prompted us to question the democratic nature of the project more deeply. We went from assessing various threats to democracy to reconceptualising how democracy itself might work. Nick, a university researcher, wondered if the project designers' ultimate accountability to the funders might require there to be limits to shared decision making:

> Could a project such as this be entirely democratic? Even if it could be, should it be? For example: Elizabeth [principal investigator], you are account-able to ESRC. If the rest of us decided democratically to negate some aspect of your contract with ESRC, that would leave you in an untenable position. I am much more certain that we can and must be clear and honest, with ourselves and each other, about where power lies and how that power is enacted through decisions. If this is always on the agenda, that will help us to clarify the spaces within which we can establish democratic ways of working, and spaces in which we can't.

Elizabeth responded by pointing out a fundamental ironic tension underpinning the project: the success of the project proposal was pre-dicated on exactly the democratic processes that Nick thought might be short-circuited by institutional accountability:

> It's a good point, Nick – there ARE places where my accountability to ESRC means I need to maintain control – BUT on the other hand, one of the things the referees for the proposal liked about the project was its design, which is fundamentally about trying to establish a sort of working democracy between people with different types of knowledge and expertise.

Later, when Elizabeth asked the teachers to help decide whether or not to accept a production company's proposal to make a documentary about the project (which was an expected outcome), Sue, a teacher re-searcher, reflected on this process:

> I did feel pleased that my views were being sought. Then, I thought that in fact the final say will have to rest with Elizabeth [principal investigator]. So, is

that democracy? It could be seen as a tokenistic gesture towards democracy. Elizabeth might care about what we think, she might not, but is that ultimate decision going to the vote? I doubt it.

Sue's characterisation of democracy as an impossible and not particularly desirable goal seemed to be closely tied with the reduction of the concept to a static and potentially tokenistic system of majority rule. Later Deb, a university researcher, refocused this notion of democracy from a static system to dynamic discursive process:

I think that when [Elizabeth] asks 'is the project democratic?' we are drawn into thinking about in/equality of power, who has and does not have it etc. A 'zero-sum' model. And as various of you have pointed out, access to resources (time, knowledge, language, budgets) means that, with this notion of power, there are inequalities (which we can then engage in dialogue over and modify our practice in order to address).

In her own academic writing, Deb has drawn upon Foucault's reformulation of power as sovereign (that 'possessed by' a leader) to a notion of disciplinary power (the discursive deployment of self-evident truths): 'One discourse in not intrinsically imbued with more or less power than another. Yet the historicity of particular discursive practices means that some discourses ... do come to dominate and bound legitimate knowledge and, indeed, what is knowable' (Youdell, 2006a:35-36). Disciplinary power can be interrupted by interrogating those truths that seem self-evident, which recasts democracy as a process rather than an ideal state of equally shared power. Wenger also situates power within a continual negotiation process: 'it requires or creates some form of consensus in order to become socially effective, but the meaning of the consensus is something whose ownership always remains open to negotiation' (1998:207). Viewed in this light, a democratic community is an emergent process of interrogation guided by the question, 'By what means do individuals come to be positioned within a group at a particular moment and over time?' (Berry, 2006:514).

Negotiating the research gaze

This section describes a particular case where participants negotiated their positioning within the group over time. Once again drawing upon Foucault, this case concerns surveillance, or the power of the anonymous gaze. Referring to the panopticon prison design[10] where one guard would be able to observe a number of individual prisoners who could see neither the guard nor the other prisoners, Foucault writes that the object of the panoptic surveillance 'is seen, but does not see; he is the object of information, never a subject in communication' (1997b: 200). In an email sent to Elizabeth, Renée and Judy (all university researchers) on September 30, 2006, Laura's description of the university-teacher relationship strongly parallels Foucault's panoptic relationship:

> I feel that although I may be researching in my classroom in relation to whatever project I develop ... I am still being researched by you whereas you can research without being researched yourself. What I say in these emails and on the discussion forum can be interpreted by you.

The teachers may be researchers, but they are under the watchful gaze of the university researchers who, as Laura puts it, enjoy the privilege of researching without being researched ... the unseen gazer. Renée's response reveals that she is still applying her early idealised notion of the project's shared practice; she suggests that while university researchers might train the research gaze on teachers, teacher researchers might just as easily train the research gaze on university members:

> Yes, this makes *a lot* of sense to me. It feels like we can go off and write our interpretations of your postings, because they're *data*. Which I have to agree feels really creepy to me ... That being said, I suppose other people on the web might want to use people's postings as data ... I think we agreed that nobody would use anybody's postings as data without first letting people know what they wanted to use them for and getting permission from the people themselves. That goes for everyone, Elizabeth A, me, teachers [university researchers], etc.

Renée failed to take into consideration some of the institutional realities described above, which make it rather unlikely that a teacher would have the time or inclination to view a university researcher as a research subject, a reality Laura gently points out in her response:

> I guess in life in general whatever anyone says or writes (or in whatever way discourse is made public) ... can be open to interpretation. But then me interpreting something someone says in a conversation is different to me interpreting it and then writing and publishing a paper on it.

While this exchange prompted Elizabeth to involve the *No Outsiders* community in the web-based discussion of democracy described above, an examination of further email communications between Laura and some of the university researchers reveals that Laura's discomfort at being the subject of the research gaze was far from resolved. In addition, we can see that our shared project focus on sexualities equality has positioned Laura in an unfamiliar and complex way in terms of her local practice community, which in turn has placed her in an awkward position in terms of the *No Outsiders* community: under what conditions might the conflict between Laura's teacher and sexual identity become *our* data, placing Laura in an even more vulnerable position under the research gaze?

A month and a half later, Laura, still concerned that she was not 'doing' enough, sent an email to Elizabeth and Renée where she critically analysed some of the personal factors that she felt might complicate her position as a *No Outsiders* teacher researcher who was not out in her school:

> Although I realise that this project is about equality rather than personal flag waving of any sort, I can't get myself out of it ... and when I begin to question its relevance, I always come back to myself and think that it's not for nothing that I feel anxious about coming out to colleagues ... I wonder how differently (or not) I'd understand this if I was straight ... And when I deal with other equalities issues I wonder how much I understand the subtler aspects of issues people face.

Focusing on Laura's concerns about 'not doing' enough, Elizabeth responded by enthusiastically supporting Laura's self-reflections as powerful data and encouraged her to post them in the section of the project website where people's data, in whatever form, were being collected and shared:

> I'm *really* glad that you feel that being a lesbian allows you to see the significance of LGBT equality and to press ahead and do something about it – it's all too often the case that gay teachers feel that they *shouldn't* address the issue, exactly because they're gay! ... This conversation ... is really valuable potential project data ... If you're happy for it (or selected bits, if you prefer) to go on the website as data, either now or in the future, that would be great.

Renée responded as well, encouraging Laura to keep self-reflecting and to consider this as a valid form of data collection:

126

> ... Good action research is very much self-reflective, so please don't feel compelled to leave yourself out of the equation. For me the weakest of action research is when people just do something and describe it, and the strongest is when people interrogate how their own identities affect and are affected by their teaching. I think you are definitely on your way to the good stuff ... Elizabeth and I have reflected rather a lot on how our identities as straight and lesbian researcher position us with respect to our work and perhaps influence our perceptions, relationships and actions.

In this posting, Renée revealed that she and Elizabeth have these same kinds of self-reflections, but at this point neither university researcher went so far as to actually share their self-reflections with Laura (Elizabeth referred to 'gay teachers' in general, and Renée mentioned only the fact that she had reflected, without giving any details). In other words, they have not yet engaged Laura personally, but only as mentors or coaches. And they have not exposed themselves to the public gaze (sharing their own self-reflections as 'data' with the rest of the team) as they recommend she does. While Renée and Elizabeth might seem a bit slow to understand what seems rather obvious in hindsight, it is probably useful to point out that both remained focused on Laura's earlier, explicitly stated concerns that thinking was not doing, which masked Laura's additional personal safety concerns until she found herself forced to state these more explicitly as well.

Laura responded by reminding the university researchers that placing one's personal life in the public gaze is risky (even theory is safer!) and tactfully suggests that *they* start the public self-reflection discussion:

> It would feel slightly different posting something like this to posting something about theory ... theory is much safer! But I agree, our own identities are central to what we are doing and interrogating all the issues that surrounds this is important – so for that reason, I feel I ought to post ... If one of you guys were to start a discussion I'd probably respond with something along the same kind of lines as what I've written here.

Elizabeth, apparently interpreting Laura's invitation to start a discussion as literally placing the words on the discussion forum, reiterates her request to upload Laura's relatively private email reflections into the public data space of the web:

> I've just had an email conversation with another teacher researcher in the project who, like you Laura, is offering some *fabulous* thought-provoking

comments through long email discussions. I've asked her – and I'd now like to ask you – for permission to put up either the whole of the email exchanges we've had – you, me, Judy, Renée – or edited highlights if you prefer ... not into the discussion forum but into the 'our project data' section of the website.

Drawing upon earlier exchanges, Elizabeth seems to have read Laura's reticence as a lingering belief that her 'thinking' was not valid data, a concern that Laura had expressed earlier. Finally, Laura abandoned her earlier tactful and discreet approach by directly stating her concerns about *who* is researching *whom* in relation to the explicit aims of the *No Outsiders* project to disrupt these very hierarchies:

> Because I care that this project is as democratic as it can be ... because it has more potential to be than other research – I'll only put stuff up about my-self if you guys [university researchers] are prepared to do the same. Other-wise it'd feel weird – like only the teacher researchers were being researched ... If you're wanting us to interrogate our own subject positions and the impact that has on our perceptions, actions etc. in relation to this project – and put our reflections about that stuff on the web – then you also must do the same ... for the sake of trying to keep things equal-ish! Do you see where I'm com-ing from? Or do you think I'm being ridiculous?

Laura retreats back to a more cautious position at the end, inviting the university researchers to decide whether they think she is being ridi-culous, but in the end she managed to disrupt research relationships that we as a team had taken for granted. By demanding that the univer-sity researchers subject themselves to the same surveillance that they expected of the teacher researchers, Laura contests and re-imagines her subject position in the *No Outsiders* community. This constitutes a renegotiation of practice: the university researchers must share the practice of being the object of research in this research community. The short term result was that Elizabeth initiated a new web discussion entitled 'Speaking as a lesbian: Researcher identities and the impact on research' where she took the lead in sharing her reflections on her posi-tion as a lesbian researcher as community data (see Chapter 7 for some of these reflections).

Later, reflecting on this experience in an email, Elizabeth explained that Laura's insistence that we (university researchers) take the lead on self-reflection constituted a turning point in her understanding of the democracy of the project and her role as principal investigator. She reflected on further risks that she took in opening additional discussions about her positioning in the project in terms of sexual history, academic identity and teaching experience, risks she would not have taken 'had it not been for Laura's early exhortation to 'you guys' to open ourselves up to critical commentary and analysis on personal issues before she would be prepared to do so herself.'

Elizabeth's description of her 'turning point' contributes to our belief that this renegotiation of community positioning constitutes, rather than reflects, our democratic process.

A 'democratic' 'community' of 'practice': from product to (unpredictable, uncomfortable, never-ending) process

Michelle Fine (1994) compares the researcher-researched relationship with other power-imbued relationships between members of dominant and marginalised racial and ethnic groups; the researcher has the power to define the research and terms of interaction. In this sense, academics' attempts to give teachers choices and voices in the research process risk belittling and essentialising them in ways similar to any attempt to 'empower' the Other. The university researchers' early attempts to encourage teacher researchers to voice their personal reflections as legitimate project data may have been just such a misguided attempt at empowerment.

Members of a research community, particularly one that self-defines as transgressing traditional researcher-subject dichotomies, will need to negotiate their unique terms of empowerment. Eisenhart exhorts us to accept the postmodern challenge of holding the tension among the various, and perhaps incompatible, perspectives that emerge through research: 'we will have to participate, along with others, with one perspective or voice among many. We will have to speak what we know and believe in, but we will also have to listen, deliberate, negotiate, and compromise around the knowledge and beliefs of others who are involved' (1999:465).

This negotiation process might not always be pleasant, particularly as it requires honest expressions of conflicting interests that tend to be subdued by dominant cultural notions of niceness that encourage us to avoid conflict (Moje, 2000). While the negotiations described in this paper were relatively congenial, this kind of honesty can lead to angry outbursts and open confrontation. Nevertheless, honest reflections on emotional responses such as anger, betrayal and frustration 'can ultimately strengthen the relationship and make it more nearly a partnership of equals' (Somekh, 2002:89). Lave identifies conflict as inherent in human joint endeavour, and specifies that this conflict tends to reflect situated interests, feelings and beliefs rather than abstract 'truth' claims:

> Analysis focused on conflictual practices of changing understanding in activity is not so likely to concentrate on the truth or error of some knowledge claim. It is more likely to explore disagreements over what is relevant; whether, and how much, something is worth knowing and doing; what to make of ambiguous circumstances; what is convenient for whom, what to do next when one does not know what to expect, and who cares most about what (1996:15).

Whether congenially or confrontationally negotiated, these disagreements cannot be silenced in the pursuit of civility or safety, but need to be continually and openly negotiated by all interested parties. Frankham and Howes (2006) emphasise process in their account of setting up a collaborative relationship between university and teacher researchers. Rather than regard disturbances as unfortunate side-effect of collaboration, they argue that knowledge cannot be separated from the processes of generating it and that these processes, enacted through talk as action, are integral to the research. Responding to McNiff's (2002) call for researchers to explore the kinds of relationships needed to produce educational knowledge, they suggest that relationships are, by their very nature, unknowable; therefore action research, reliant on particular relationships that develop in specific context, must be constantly reinvented (Frankham and Howes, 2006).

Yet the very understanding that relationships are negotiated through (sometimes uncomfortable and conflicting) dialogue with an unknowable, unfinalisable (Bakhtin, 1999) Other might help us enter into dialogic relationships with our research partners. While this might satisfy McNiff's call for a 'kind of relationship,' it is the kind of relationship that recognises its unknowability right from the start. Given this unknowability, we cannot provide guidelines or a list of 'best practice' for democratic community building, but we can share some insights that have arisen in the building of our own community:

- Communities of practice are dynamic and emergent, and neither stable nor predictable. As Wenger writes, 'There is an inherent uncertainty between design and its realisation in practice, since practice is not the result of design but rather a response to it' (1998:233).

- Participants in practice communities will have different goals and understandings which must come to bear in negotiations of meaning. In our case, situated understandings were shaped by our current (sometimes conflicting) responsibilities to other practice communities as well as different personal histories. We discovered this complexity in practice, as conflicts emerged.

- There is an element of trust involved in revealing our understandings to each other (Laura had to trust Elizabeth and Renée enough to reveal the source of her discomfort, and Elizabeth had to trust the team enough to initiate discussions of her own sexual identity in relation to the project). Just because our web discussion forum was password-protected doesn't mean we necessarily felt safe with each other. This trust emerges as relationships develop, and cannot be taken for granted.

- Keeping dialogue alive is essential to any community of practice, but particularly to one devoted to innovation and transformation of practice. An important challenge for the *No Outsiders* team has been resisting the temptation to smooth over our differences, 'Blending, somehow, always ends up privileging the perspective of the blade' (Wenger, 1998:256).

We are not saying that we have completely succeeded in following our own advice; our relationships are certainly not entirely open and trusting, and no relationship is ever fully dialogic. Nevertheless, we suggest that researchers consider democracy as process and engage each in constant reflexive dialogue without fear of the unknown or disruptive.

Note

10 The panopticon was designed by Jeremy Bentham but never instituted. Foucault related in an interview that the early 19th century prison design projects he studied invariably made reference to Bentham's panopticon (Foucault, 1974).

9

No Outsiders: Exploring transformations at the intersections of communities of practice

Elizabeth Brace

Like DePalma and Teague, Brace explores how Wenger's concept of communities of practice, upon which the project was designed, has shaped the development of the project. While DePalma and Teague focus primarily on internal dynamics, Brace explores the ways in which the complex and fluid community of practice which constituted the *No Outsiders* project overlapped and intersected with a range of other communities, examining both the benefits and tensions of these overlaps. She focuses in particular on two instances of opposition to the project's work which drew on faith-based communities of practice in different contexts. Brace demonstrates how the sometimes difficult negotiations that occur across boundaries where communities of practice 'have nudged up against and overlapped other communities' can provide opportunities for transformation.

Introduction

As Groundwater-Smith and Mockler (2005) argue, practitioner research should be transformative in intent and action. Based on a participatory action research (PAR) model, the *No Outsiders* project aimed to effect political change. One of its two stated objectives was 'to create a community of practice within which teachers can develop effective approaches to addressing sexualities equality within the broader context of inclusive education' (extract from the funding bid). The project design included plans to create an alliance between academics and teachers who, as a wider team working across three regions in England, would form a single community of practice (Lave and Wenger, 1991; Wenger, 1998). With its agenda to effect change, it was hoped that this community of practice would act as what Somekh (2005) describes as a global action research community, which might genuinely have the power to inform policy and practice within and beyond the project schools.

This community of practice was explicitly conceptualised in terms of the relationships among *No Outsiders* team members and particularly the relationships between university and teacher researchers. While the project's stated aims were to effect change beyond the project, the ways in which *No Outsiders* as a community of practice might relate politically to other communities of practice was not stated (see DePalma, in press, however, for a post-hoc account). The nature and degree of these changes has been largely unanticipated. Here I explore aspects of this process.

I begin with the concept of a community of practice, particularly in relation to Wenger's description of constellations of overlapping communities of practice (1998). The focus moves to the many ways in which *No Outsiders* has fruitfully related to and worked with and alongside other communities. Finally, I look at two examples of the tensions this process can evoke. Such tensions have presented challenges, but they have been productive too, compelling us to examine and re-examine our aims with reference to our positionings within multiple communities.

What is a community of practice and what are constellations?

The notion of 'communities of practice' has been taken up broadly across the social, educational and management sciences (Barton and Tusting, 2005) and was developed in particular by Jean Lave and Etienne Wenger in their book *Situated Learning: Legitimate peripheral participation* (1991). Legitimate peripheral participation suggests that knowledge is not simply transferred from what Lave and Wenger term 'masters' or 'old-timers' and assimilated by 'newcomers' or 'apprentices', but that learning represents a complex process involving individuals' trajectories through communities of practice. While learning is often imagined as separate from and even contrasting with practice,

Lave and Wenger's sociocultural understanding of learning re-casts it as a feature of all practice, which emerges as members negotiate their engagement in a shared practice. Hildreth and Kimble describe communities of practice as 'vehicles' for learning (2008:ix).

Wenger (1998) subsequently took these ideas forward, particularly the concept of communities of practice, exploring the social relationships associated with them (Hughes *et al*, 2007a). In his later work, Wenger uses the concept more widely than in his work with Lave, including in the 'knowledge-intensive workplace' (Hughes *et al*, 2007a:3). While his later work has been seen as lacking 'critical edge' (Barton and Tusting, 2005:6), Wenger does move the work forward in crucial ways.

Wenger elaborates on how meaning is produced within communities of practice, refering specifically to the roles of participation and reification in this process. He uses the term 'participation' to relate to both action and connection: for him, the term refers to 'a process of taking part and also to the relations with others that reflect that process' (1998:55). The meanings that are negotiated within a community of practice involve both participation and what he calls 'reification.' Wenger states:

> I refer to the process of giving form to our experience by producing objects that congeal this experience into 'thingness.' In so doing we create points of focus around which the negotiation of meaning becomes organised ... Writing down a law, creating a procedure, or producing a tool is a similar process. (*ibid*:58)

However, such objects or tools can take on a life of their own. Using the example of the workplace statement of values, this does not necessarily mean that the values within it are reflected in practice: it can become, or is in a sense already, divorced from its origins. Further, 'reification as a constituent of meaning is always incomplete, ongoing, potentially enriching, and potentially misleading' (*ibid*:62). Wenger sees participation and reification, then, as complementary processes through which meaning is negotiated in any community of practice, 'Negotiated meaning is at once both historical and dynamic, contextual and unique' (*ibid*:54). What varies from community to community is, therefore, the degree to which one or the other process is dominant.

Secondly, as Lave and Wenger suggest, communities of practice overlap with 'other tangential and overlapping communities of practice' (1991:

98). As such, they 'constitute a complex social landscape of shared practices, boundaries, peripheries, overlaps, connections, and encounters' (Wenger, 1998:118), and it is this aspect of communities of practice that I focus on here. Wenger introduces the term 'constellations' to refer to these communities and to the 'constellations of interconnected practices' associated with them:

> constellation refers to a grouping of stellar objects that are seen as a configuration even though they may not be particularly close to one another, of the same kind, or of the same size. A constellation is a particular way of seeing them as related, one that depends on the perspective one adopts.' (*ibid*: 127)

Wenger gives a range of reasons for why communities might form a constellation, including:

> shared historical roots; having related enterprises; serving a cause or belonging to an institution; facing similar conditions; having members in common; sharing artifacts; having geographical relations of proximity or interaction; having overlapping styles or discourses; competing for the same resources. (*ibid*:127)

He usefully explores what happens at the boundaries and peripheries of communities where they overlap with others and, in doing so, connect with them. For Wenger boundaries represent closure and discontinuity; peripheries imply openness and continuity. As he suggests, 'joining a community of practice involves entering not only its internal configuration, but also its relations with the rest of the world' (*ibid*:103). Wenger uses the concept of 'brokering' to describe the way in which people take elements from one community of practice into another. Where communities connect, he uses the term 'boundary objects' to describe the way in which the artefacts and concepts associated with one community of practice might cross from one to another, or link one with another. Returning to the notion of reification, such objects and the way in which they are understood can be reified by other individuals and groups beyond the community of practice that gave birth to them. Meaning can change in reification, as I go on to discuss.

There have been a number of valid criticisms of Lave and Wenger's work on communities of practice. Critics have identified a lack of clarity about what falls inside and what falls outside communities of practice.

Some have commented on the ahistoricity of the model (Engeström, 2007; Jewson, 2007), its lack of attention to power (Barton and Hamilton, 2005; Hughes *et al*, 2007a; Engeström, 2007; Jewson, 2007), the tensions within communities of practice (Fuller, 2007; Jewson, 2007), the influence of social divisions (Hughes *et al*, 2007b) and its inherently non-transformative nature (Fuller, 2007; Jewson, 2007).

My analysis also focuses on this last criticism: that the community of practice is by nature not transformative. This is important in light of our own deliberately transformative aims. Commenting on Lave and Wenger's conceptualisation of learning in general, Jewson (2007) argues that both Lave and Wenger (1991) and Wenger's (1998) work lack focus on innovation due to its emphasis on the replication of existing practice. In this way communities of practice might arguably be static (Fuller, 2007): although there are newcomers to the practice, the practice itself does not change.

On the other hand, Schwier and Daniel argue that 'communities are not static; they shift, morph, and undulate, sometimes in unpredictable ways' (2008:356). Arguably, Lave and Wenger's work, with its focus on social processes, suggests this. They state that: 'since activity and the participation of individuals involved in it, their knowledge, and their perspectives are mutually constitutive, change is a fundamental property of communities of practice' (Lave and Wenger, 1991:117).

DePalma (in press) suggests that Wenger's (1998) most widely read work, which takes a group of people working in an insurance company as its example of a community of practice, has reinforced the notion of a group of people working towards replication rather than change. However, DePalma argues that communities of practice just 'are' – they are not inherently transformational, or indeed, reproductive but they do have the potential to be so, depending on their context and nature. She has illustrated how this has taken place in relation to *No Outsiders*, expanding our understandings of how communities of practice might operate. As she suggests, the project itself has been involved in the transformation, rather than the reproduction, of teaching and research practices. While the potential for transformation has usually been associated with what happens within a community of practice, our own aims have been to effect transformation beyond *No Outsiders'* borders. However, this process has not been unproblematic.

Mapping out communities

The community of practice that is *No Outsiders* has developed into a web of relationships that has become increasingly complex and extensive. While connections with other groups was certainly anticipated and planned, the various ways in which we, as a community of practice, have nudged up against and overlapped other communities to form various constellations has sometimes been unexpected. In addition, relationships were often built through organic processes whereby strategic connections were made across and between different individuals and groups as the potential or need for them arose.

While institutions or labelled groups do not in themselves represent communities of practice, where aims and practices are shared by people who operate *within* these institutions or groups, single or multiple communities of practice can arguably exist within them. The multiple groups and communities of practice we have had contact with, and formed constellations with, both as individual researchers and as a wider project, include:

■ *Local authority representatives*
  A number of local authorities (LAs) have made efforts to adopt or mirror project work in their local institutional contexts. Their approaches range from inviting *No Outsiders* project teachers to present workshops at school or authority-level professional development events to more elaborate mentoring schemes, such as partnering LA schools with *No Outsiders* schools.

■ *Academics*
  Groups of like-minded academics have supported us in disseminating our work via seminars, conferences, newsletters, collaborative publications, etc. These include research groups situated within academic institutions, such as the Centre for the Interdisciplinary Study of Sexuality and Gender in Europe, based at the University of Exeter, and the Centre for Equalities and Social Justice, based at the University of Sunderland. They also include pan-institutional special interest groups (SIGs), such as the Queer Studies SIG of the American Educational Research Association (AERA) and the Sexualities SIG of the British Educational research Association (BERA).

138

■ *Arts workers*

We have worked with a number of arts workers and groups, many of whom have done multiple projects with the same project schools or worked across several project schools. Some have worked nationally with project schools in different regions, including an actor/writer/poet and a film company that has been documenting the project's activities.

■ *Activist groups*

Activist groups have been involved in the project, and some members have acted in an advisory capacity. Throughout the project we have continued to develop such contacts.

■ *Teaching colleagues, school governors, parents, and children*

As expected, contact with these groups has been considerable, due to the nature of practitioner research: individual teacher researchers in particular have acted as contact points or brokers in relation to the project, with immediate colleagues and others, both inside their schools and beyond.

It is particularly difficult to determine whether *No Outsiders* begins and ends with the core group of university and teacher researchers or whether it expands, as the boundaries blur, where arts workers, activists, local authorities, teachers' colleagues, parents and children work with us as (sometimes unwitting) allies. This is particularly so where people use the title *No Outsiders* in their schools to describe a philosophy or as a title for their inclusion week, or a local authority runs a *No Outsiders* day: both of which have happened during the course of the project. It is also anticipated that when the project funding ends, the work that has been done will continue. Teachers themselves will continue their work and may even continue to see themselves as a defined group. Some local authorities are already looking at ways of replicating the project in their schools. In this sense *No Outsiders*, while a bounded 28 month project, continues and expands, but not necessarily in a form that its originators intended or had control over.

While communities of practice are most often conceptualised as working inwards – individuals working at the periphery move towards the centre of the community or towards mastery – our aims to transform practice beyond our own community of practice into others can more accurately be described as pushing awareness, understanding and knowledge of sexualities equality outwards. There are many ways in which, via the work of individuals as brokers, we have worked across the borders between our own community of practice and others. For example, one teacher researcher has developed teaching resources that have been widely taken up by teachers outside the project. These materials act as what Wenger (1998) calls boundary objects that span the divide between communities. Similarly, another teacher researcher has been asked to act as a case study for equalities workers and other teachers to learn from, and many of the teacher researchers have been invited to talk about their work in other practice settings.

It is important to keep in mind that the mere fact of having a *No Outsiders* teacher based at a school does not imply that the entire school, or even the head teacher, might be considered to belong to the *No Outsiders* community of practice or even support it. Any given school will support a complex array of interacting and sometimes conflicting communities, requiring constant negotiation between *No Outsiders* and schools where members are based. For example, one teacher researcher in the project worked hard to reconcile her own strong belief in the project's aims with the less than enthusiastic response to the project from her colleagues and also the head teacher. It was only when a project head teacher from a different school visited to show a film of her school's inclusion week that these colleagues began to voice their support for addressing sexualities. Crucially, the head decided to include project books into the literacy spine and the subject of sexualities explicitly within the school's own inclusion week. Although in this instance the head acted as an additional broker for the project by supporting its work, this was at best a temporary role: as the teacher researcher went on to say afterwards, the steps forward taken in her school, and by her head, were sometimes followed by steps backward. This is only one example of how particular teacher researchers, acting as brokers between communities, sometimes sat uneasily with their feet in two different camps with, at times, different aims and objectives.

More widely the project has had impact as an entity in itself. Returning to Wenger's concept of reification, the project title, which itself reifies a statement by Desmond Tutu that there are 'no outsiders' regardless of beliefs, colour, gender or sexuality, has been reified by people and organisations beyond the project. For some it has come to represent sexualities equality work in primary schools *per se*. There are a number of local authorities keen to associate themselves with the project: it seems that beyond simply drawing on the knowledge we have acquired, such affiliation appears to act as a symbol of their own commitment to sexualities equality. For example, Newcastle City Council's 2008-9 *Sexual Orientation Equality Plan*[11] includes a statement that it is seeking affiliation with the project as part of a public statement detailing how they are addressing sexualities equality. The issue with such reification is the way in which the meanings associated with the object in question – in this case the label or symbol *No Outsiders* – can change, as DePalma (in press) has highlighted. I return to this issue later.

While it is true that we have influenced and supported others, it is also important to acknowledge that others have influenced and supported us. The connection we made with *Gendered Intelligence*, an organisation promoting the rights of transgender and gender variant youth, affected our work particularly meaningfully. The relationship both challenged and changed our own understandings of what transgender meant, and how that related to gender and sexuality and to notions of fixed and fluid identities. The resulting increased awareness in our negotiation of these already-contested borders has deepened our understanding of the difficulties and complexities associated with this work. The association has also had an impact on some project schools which chose to take up specific work on gender identity. In a way which was echoed in other collaborations, we came to see Jay Stewart, the cofounder of *Gendered Intelligence* who worked closely with us and led workshops in some project schools, as an essential member of the *No Outsiders* team.

A powerful example of how the communities of others overlapped our own to mutual benefit and in a way that blurs the boundaries between them is illustrated by Roy, a member of a drama group that worked with one of the project schools during their inclusion weeks both in the first and second years of the project. Initially, Roy felt hesitant when he and his group were asked to address sexualities as part of their work with us. He reflected on his initial concerns in one of the project documentary films:

I came to the project a year ago ... and I thought, 'I'm not touching this with a barge pole!' It's – you know, it's a, a no-go area, it's going to cause all sorts of problems, parents aren't going to like it when you're talking to children about homosexuality, or transgender ... and I just thought, 'No, I'm not going to do that'. And [the teacher researcher] gave me some books, some children's books to read and we read the books and we thought, 'I don't really ... it's not what we're going to do.' And then, I've got a 10 year-old daughter, she came home and she saw these books and she read a couple of the books and she said to me, 'We can't have these in the house.' I said, 'Why can't we have these in the house?' And she said, 'Well, people might think we're gay or something.' And I realised in that moment that at 10 years old, she was already being bombarded with peer pressure; she'd already realised and made her mind up that gay is bad and we can't go there, and I thought, 'Well, if at this age they're already saying that we can't accept people for their life choices, then we have to start educating them earlier.' That was when I realised what [the teacher researcher] was trying to do and I thought, 'Well, I have to get involved.'

Roy's statements that he 'came to the project' and 'I have to get involved' suggest more than simply working with *No Outsiders* from the outside: he saw himself as committed to our aims and practices. His use of the shared repertoires and boundary objects associated with the project, such as the project books, and the way in which he worked with teacher researchers to deliver workshops that met the aims of the project also point to this, albeit temporary, belonging. This attitude will have certainly influenced other members of his drama group, reflected both in his willingness to act as their representative on film and in his own response to my request for permission to use his words here: in an email he made it clear that he and his group were proud to be named in relation to their *No Outsiders*-related work. Roy's own community of practice effectively overlapped our own, and blurred the boundaries between the two.

Working with dissensus?

As DePalma (in press) suggests, Wenger's (1998) description of the import and export of practices fails to capture the way in which practice is also exercised in peripheral spaces between us and others in a complex process of developing shared understandings. Wenger himself suggests that it is at the boundaries of communities of practice and in the overlap with other communities of practice that meanings associated with those communities can change. While this can be positive for the communities that intersect, there is the potential for meanings to change in less positive ways, and this can lead to either a breakdown in negotiations and relations or to further focused negotiations involving participants whose prior exclusion had supported a false sense of resolution.

Further, while Wenger's boundary objects can prove useful ways of exporting ideas, utilising them in different practices can be risky. For example, the term 'sexualities' is commonly employed in academic circles to avoid essentialising identity categories such as 'lesbian' or 'gay'. But this was not easily imported into primary education contexts. The use of the term 'sexualities' was questioned by some primary practitioners and social activists because of its implied reference to sex – particularly problematic given the sexualisation of gay, lesbian and bisexual people (Ellis and High, 2004; DePalma and Atkinson, 2006) and the way in which children are constructed as innocent (Epstein and Johnson, 1998), making discussion of sexual identities with young children seem inappropriate. However, the use of 'LGBT' (as imported from much current activist practice) was seen by some team members to be less than inclusive – what about the straights, queers, questioning and intersex...?

The term 'homophobia' was strategically imported from current government (as well as some media) discourse reflecting recent attention to homophobia and homophobic bullying as a way to render it recognisable and legitimate for teachers. However, one teacher researcher suggested that it might be problematic in that some of the families in her school community would link this word to homosexuality and its promotion, which, she felt, they would view negatively. This illustrates that even within the same institution, importing terms or boundary objects across professional and social communities can be tricky. The varied understandings of these terms, based on pre-existing assumptions and personal histories, meant that as boundary objects they might fail to express the project's aims or, worse, prejudice people against it.

While Lave and Wenger (1991) and Wenger (1998) refer to tensions that might occur within communities of practice, little attention is given to how these operate in relation to other communities of practice or how communities of practice operate in constellations. I explore two of the ways in which our work has overlapped with particular faith communities and the tensions associated with this overlap.

The first relates to the concerns of a largely Somali Muslim community had about the project and how our own community of practice negotiated these concerns. For the sake of brevity, I describe the perspectives of the various communities and organisations (*No Outsiders*, parents, local council, etc.) in general terms, but there were complex dynamics within and across the groups. Early in the project's second year, families with children in one of the schools that had recently joined expressed concern about its *No Outsiders* work. They objected that there had been a lack of consultation on the use of project materials, including the children's books provided by the project. The objections were based on parents' perceived rights and on the community's religious faith: one representative from the community – Farooq Siddique, community development officer for Bristol Muslim Cultural Society, governor at the school, and *Bristol Evening Post* columnist – told the BBC: 'In Islam homosexual relationships are not acceptable' (Siddique, 2008).

While families and community representatives agreed that homophobia should be tackled, they were unhappy with the project's more proactive approach where lesbian, gay and bisexual people, identities, and relationships were being discussed. Siddique said that:

> The agenda was to reduce homophobic bullying, and all the parents said they were not against that side of it, but families were saying to us 'Our child is coming home and talking about same-sex relationships, when we haven't talked about heterosexual relationships with them yet ... it appears the primary schools are operating under the premise that to challenge homophobia it is necessary to explain what homophobia is. (*ibid*)

Siddique made further reference in the media to the concerns of parents that children's innocence was being threatened and the parents' prioritisation of academic subjects over 'homosexuality' (*ibid*). These responses to the project's work echo those we have encountered during the project and elsewhere.

Feelings ran high after the radio broadcast. Some members of the community picketed the school and tried to send children home. The local council became involved and sanctioned the removal of the project-related books from the school, since these were at the centre of parents' concerns and because the safety of staff and public would, they believed, be facilitated by the books' withdrawal. Several community meetings were held to try and work through the tensions, which were still not fully resolved at the time of writing. However, negotiations have not reached the point of breakdown and are being taken forward by, among others, the local LGB activist/support group. Time will tell whether negotiations will indeed break down now that *No Outsiders* is no longer officially involved.

Significantly, a local council representative recently informed us that any further sexualities work in schools would have to continue without the label 'No Outsiders', as this, she argued, had become too inflammatory. As a term that has acquired particular connotations within a particular history of border negotiation, it has been rejected as boundary object as the borders between the *No Outsiders* community and the local communities are closed down. Nevertheless, the local council has made a strategic move in an attempt to facilitate negotiations around the actual practices initiated by the *No Outsiders* community, suggesting a possibility that a transformation of practice may continue beyond the officially recognised intersection of communities.

The second example relates to the setting up of an equalities group in one of the project schools, with an agenda to address multiple equalities. It was partly funded by *No Outsiders* and members included parents, governors and teachers, with a parent-governor as the Chair. Tensions arose early – in the first meeting – when two of the parents objected to the inclusion of sexualities equality on the group's agenda on Christian grounds. As before, representation was raised as an issue:

> [One of the two parents who opposed sexualities work] felt she hadn't been fully represented in the minutes of the previous meeting, and that some people had treated her differently since that meeting. The second part I'm sure is probably true? It's hard for people to be as open and friendly when they feel someone has fundamentally different ideas from their own. (Teacher researcher journal)

While these parents, like the Somali Muslim parents, acknowledged that homophobia should be tackled, they objected to the exploration of sexualities equality with children of primary school age:

It's so frustrating to have lots of people full of energy and enthusiasm blocked by two people ... They insist ... that they have nothing against homosexuals, but don't want their children to hear any mention of them when so young. Substitute Black: 'I have nothing against Black people, it's just that I think children need to be older before they hear about them...' (Teacher researcher journal)

The confusion of children in relation to having to navigate these different kinds of relationships was referred to, and the two parents used their Christian beliefs to support their arguments. One of them implied that she represented the wider Christian community in her view that same-sex relationships were unacceptable. Yet many of others in the group were Christians, and they questioned this parent's claim to represent their religion. When the protesting parent tried to support her arguments by reading passages of the Bible relating to same-sex relationships, this was strongly objected to by the others. Except for the two parents, all the members of the group – some gay, some straight, some Christian, some not – argued strongly against the school excluding sexualities equality issues. Many were upset and angry that their own or their friends' sexual identities were seen as less valid than other sexualities.

Clearly, what equalities actually meant was contested in this setting, despite the supposedly cohesive joint enterprise of addressing multiple equalities areas. And the *No Outsiders* community of practice, with its own understandings of what equalities include, overlapped uncomfortably with the equalities group community of practice, whose membership included individuals whose understanding of 'legitimate' equalities differed from ours and from that of other members of the group.

While both sets of objectors referred to the notion of parental rights, and to the way in which proactive sexualities equality work threatened the innocence of children, religion appeared in both cases to be the bedrock from which parents concerns arose. However, this supposedly unifying factor perhaps obscured the way in which the Muslims and Christians involved did not necessarily represent their wider communities, and the fact that these wider communities did not consist only of people who shared the same opinions on how sexualities equality should be addressed in schools. Such complexity and multiplicity of

146

opinion has not necessarily been represented in the media, which has tended to identify two apparently opposing groups. Early press articles suggested that Christian organisations opposed the *No Outsiders* project, although at this point such opposition was not evident. Later, when the *Daily Mail* misrepresented an academic conference planned by *No Outsiders* group members, another newspaper cast the issue as a conflict between religion and homophobia, announcing that: 'An academic conference organised by a group that works to combat homophobic bullying in schools has been attacked by fundamentalist Christians' (Grew, 2008). While Christian parents strategically drew upon a reified (if not universally recognised) notion of religious doctrine to support their rejection of sexualities as a legitimate equality area, this reification was all too readily taken up by the media, who seemed eager to portray pitched battles between clearly-defined and essentially opposing communities.

Similarly, when Bristol City Council liaised with *No Outsiders* and the Somali families, a commentator on a report in the *Daily Mail* appeared to rejoice at the prospect of this (mythical) pitched battle, stating that: 'The trendy do-gooders don't know which way to turn! They love to ram the gay movement down everyone's throat, but don't want to offend Muslims' (Clark, 2008).

The tendency to focus on these divisions has jeopardised the brokering process between ourselves and others and has obscured the complex picture of our relationships with people of faith and faith groups. We have had both supporters of faith and non-religious opponents. One of the project schools is run by a Muslim head teacher and we have had the support of a Muslim academic during our negotiations with the Somali parents, who spent time with us explaining how same-sex relationships are viewed and understood by his faith. Nevertheless, the fact that we have made relatively fewer connections with Muslims and Muslim organisations may have made it easier for us to cast them as the Other. It is crucial to see religious groups not as fixed and unified entities, but as shifting and multiple practice communities working within broader institutional contexts. These religious communities are constantly negotiating their practice in terms of their institutional context as well as in relation to the communities with which they overlap, and *No Outsiders* is one of these. *No Outsiders* has been working at a variety of intersections with multiple, often changing, communities of practice that may not always cohere.

While work at these intersections has been challenging, their effects have often impelled us to change and grow as a community of practice. The project has responded to the two examples described here – in the main – agreeing to try and work with, rather than against, those who are uncomfortable with our work. As a teacher researcher commented early on about the reactions in the project web discussion forum: 'I think the 'us' and 'them' categorisation would be reductive'. Kate, the teacher researcher working with the equalities group, said this on the matter:

> Perhaps we can find a way forward to work together, but it will need the two opponents of same sex relationships to realise that we are trying to be inclusive and supportive of all minority groups – and not trying to promote homosexuality over all other lifestyles, and will require the rest of us to back down from seeing them as the enemy. (Research journal)

Others have pointed to the complexity in people's positionings, in terms of both identity and beliefs:

> The ... nuanced dynamic needs to sustain us and nurture us, so that it cannot be simply depicted as warring factions. All 'communities' are intersected with fault lines that zigzag down their length; and all our identities are intersected. (University researcher, web posting)

This approach has worked with varying results. The two Christian parents described above chose to resign from the multiple equalities group and move their children into other schools. This represents a closing down of communications and of the potential inherent in the overlaps between our communities.

In the other school, negotiations continue. These may allow for a moving forward in the Muslim parents' understanding of our work and in the project team's understandings of the parents' perspectives. However, *No Outsiders* will no longer be directly involved, and the project name, which has acquired a reified meaning within the local community that we had not anticipated, will not be uttered. But teachers who once straddled the boundaries between local practice and *No Outsiders* practice remain, and their practice has been transformed by this multi-membership in ways that imply new trajectories within their

148

local practice. Boundary objects such as materials may still find their way into the schools, and our aims may still be reflected.

It is worth noting that negotiations of the kind that arose in the cases described here and elsewhere in the project had not taken place before. Here, two previously silent communities, the Somali Muslim community and the local LGB community, both of which represent wider groups traditionally marginalised in the UK state education sector, are now engaged in dialogue. The silence has been broken, with concerns surfacing and being discussed openly and, hopefully, constructively. The events will have compelled the local authority to think carefully about how such work, increasingly required as part of wider policy, is conducted in its schools. Thus the direct impact of *No Outsiders* teachers' work and its effect on the wider community may prove to be enduring, perhaps the more because of the concerns it raised.

It is unlikely that the benefits that we, *No Outsiders*, have gained from negotiations will be lost. Working with other communities, particularly in moments of tension, has caused us to think and rethink not only how we do sexualities work within the project but also the wider implications, both theoretical and in practice. This has been evident in our web-based discussions, but it is also true that as individuals we will surely carry with us the valuable insights into such border work that we have gained from these difficult processes.

Conclusion

Our own experience demonstrates that communities of practice do have the potential to be transformative. This has been seen in terms of our influence on others, causing them to take on similar aims, to adopt *No Outsiders* as a tag, or to rethink how to view sexualities and its relationship with equalities. So we have achieved some of the political change we sought. However, this work has also transformed us, both as a team and as individuals. Our aims, knowledge and understanding have all been challenged and moved on by our experiences in the project.

Through this process it has become clear that where *No Outsiders* might seem to be working in opposition to other communities within constellations of practice, apparent conflicts may act to shift the *status quo*, for example by facilitating or even forcing dialogue with previously silent groups. The neat picture of communities of practice as discrete groups that sometimes overlap or compete is challenged. It has become clear that constellations of such communities of practice operate in complex ways. The boundaries between communities blur and overlap; we intersect in many ways and on many levels. We are individuals who are also members of multiple groups; communities of practice are not homogenous but are locked in a process of change. Development and intersections between these multiple communities are not fixed – they shift according to context.

Another important aspect of the work has been the way in which the use of boundary objects, as well as the processes of reification, some-times compels us to let go of the work that we have started or the mean-ings associated with it. The meanings we have given to our work have the potential to break down when they reach our borders. Although we can work towards managing that process, we have had to accept that we cannot control it. This is particularly salient as we near the (official) end of the project.

Note
11   http://www.newcastle.gov.uk/wwwfileroot/cxo/equality/SOEPlan.pdf (p6-7).

Acknowledgements
I would like to thank the editors for their help and support during the develop-ment of this chapter, and Renée DePalma in particular for her input on the nature of communities of practice.

Notes on contributors

Alexandra Allan is a Lecturer in Education Studies in the School of Education and Lifelong Learning at the University of Exeter. Her research interests include gender, sexuality, childhood, social class, private education and single-sex schooling. Her publications include: 'The importance of being a lady: hyper-femininity and heterosexuality in the private, single-sex primary school' (*Gender and Education,* 2009) and 'Bright and Beautiful: high achieving girls, ambivalent femininities and the feminization of success in the primary school' (with Emma Renold, *Discourse,* 2006). Her current empirical research focuses on young middle-class girls' experiences of the private education system and their perceptions of risk.

Elizabeth Atkinson was a Reader in Social and Educational Inquiry and Co-Director of the Centre for Equalities and Social Justice (CESOJ) at the University of Sunderland. She has published widely on lesbian, gay, bisexual and transgender identities and equalities in primary school settings and in 2007 was awarded the Queer Studies Scholar Activist award by the Queer Studies Special Interest Group of the American Educational Research Association. Elizabeth is the Director of the ESRC-funded *No Outsiders* project, which is the focus of this book.

Elizabeth Brace was the North East university-based research assistant on the No Outsiders project. She recently completed her PhD at Newcastle University in the UK. Based primarily on interviews with women labeled as having a learning disability living in the north east of England, her PhD research focused on the ways in which the social norms associated with the intersection of gender, sexuality and 'learning disability' impact on people's lives. Prior to this Elizabeth worked in the social services and voluntary sector. Her professional and research interests centre on equalities issues in relation to gender, sexuality and disability.

Fin Cullen works as a lecturer in Youth Work studies at Brunel University. From 2007- 2009 she was involved in the *No Outsiders* project as a Research Officer based at the Institute of Education, London. Her academic work has centred on children and young people's cultures and issues of gender and sexuality. Since the early nineties, she has worked as a youth worker, and continues to manage and develop UK-based youth projects.

Renée DePalma received her PhD in 2003 from the University of Delaware (US), where she helped establish the university-community partnership *La Red Mágica* with the Latin American Community Center in Wilmington, Delaware. She worked from 2004-2009 at the University of Sunderland (UK) in sexualities equality research and was Senior Researcher for the *No Outsiders* project. Her research and teaching has focused on social justice and equity in terms of ethnicity, language, race, gender and sexuality. She is currently book reviews editor for the journal *Power and Education* and holds a research fellowship at the University of Vigo, Spain.

Judy Hemingway is a lecturer in the Department of Geography, Enterprise, Mathematics and Science at the Institute of Education, University of London. She is a geography educator whose research interests are concerned with space, place and learning. Judy's cross-disciplinary work, which interrogates the interfaces between school and academic geography, makes special reference to developments in social and cultural geography and critical pedagogy. While her recent cross-disciplinary research has focused on the spatial politics of sex and relationships education, Judy's broader interest is in the lifeworlds of young people.

Andrew Moffat has taught in primary education since 1995 as a class teacher, a teacher in a behaviour unit, in a Nurture group and a as deputy head. In 2003 he received a Masters in Teaching children with Educational and Behavioural Difficulties and he became an AST in behaviour management and inclusion the following year. Andrew has written an emotional literacy scheme of work for the primary school and has been commissioned to write similar schemes of work to promote healthy relationships, pupil voice and challenging racism. In 2007 he wrote the resource 'Challenging homophobia in early years' for his TLA stage 4 assignment, which was accredited by the GTC in 2009. By March 2009 schools in 24 different Local Authorities were using this resource.

David Nixon was awarded a PhD in theology from the University of Exeter (UK) in 2002, and is currently working as an Anglican parish priest in Plymouth. He has worked in Exeter as a University Teaching Fellow, focusing on issues of gender, power and sexuality, and was Associate Research Fellow covering SW England for the *No Outsiders* project. He has both an academic interest and practical engagement in issues of marginalization, stemming from his work with homeless people (the subject of his doctorate). He is presently exploring the stories of sexual minorities in education and the church and continues to research and write in these fields.

Susan Talburt is associate professor and director of the Women's Studies Institute at Georgia State University in Atlanta. She has published in the fields of curriculum studies, qualitative research, higher education, and gay and lesbian studies. Her books include *Subject to Identity: Knowledge, sexuality, and academic practices in higher education* (2000), the co-edited *Thinking Queer: Sexuality, culture, and education* (2000), and the co-edited *Youth and Sexualities: Pleasure, subversion, and insubordination in and out of schools* (2004).

Laura Teague has worked in primary education for the past four years and is currently a classroom teacher in a North London school. In her role as equality and diversity coordinator, she has written policies, supported staff and worked with parents to promote issues around race, disability, gender and sexualities equality. She participated in the *No Outsiders* project from 2006-2009 where she contributed to research papers and took a leading role in implementing the project in school.

Deborah Youdell is Professor of Education at the Institute of Education, University of London. Her work is located in the Sociology of Education and is concerned with educational inequalities in relation to race, gender, sexuality, religion, social class, ability and disability and the way these are connected to student subjectivities and everyday life in schools. Deborah is co-author of the award-winning *Rationing Education: policy, practice, reform and equity* and author of *Impossible Bodies, Impossible Selves: exclusions and student subjectivities*. Her latest book, *Becoming Radical*, will be published later this year. She is Regional Editor of the *International Journal of Qualitative Studies in Education* and is on the Editorial Boards of the *British Journal of Sociology of Education, Race Ethnicity Education*, and *Critical Studies in Education*.

Acknowledgements

Chapter 5 originally appeared under the same title in *Sex Education*, 8(3) p315-328 (2008) and is reprinted here with permission. An earlier version was presented at the Place-Based Sex/Sexualities and Relationship Education Conference, University of London Institute of Education 23 May 2007.

Chapter 8 appeared under the same title in *Educational Action Research* 16(4) p441-456 (2008) and is reprinted here with permission.

Earlier versions of Chapters 3 and 8 were presented at the annual meeting of the British Educational Research Association, University of London Institute of Education, 5-8 September 2007, Chapter 3 as *Queer classrooms? The possibilities for post-structural pedagogies in primary schools* and Chapter 8 as *A democratic community of practice: unpicking all those words.*

Earlier versions of Chapters 2 and 9 were presented at the annual meeting of the British Educational Research Association, Heriot-Watt University, 3-6 September 2008, Chapter 2 as *Seeking a queer pedagogic praxis: Adventures in the primary classroom* and Chapter 9 as *No Outsiders: a complex and ever-expanding community of practice.*

Earlier versions of Chapters 6 and 7 were presented at the Queering the Body; Queering Primary Education seminar, University of Exeter, 16 September 2008, Chapter 6 as *Queering the body; queering primary education: new imaginaries and new realities*; and Chapter 7 as *Bodies and minds: strategic essentialism and political activism in sexualities equality work in the primary school.*

References

Airton, L (2009) From sexuality (gender) to gender (sexuality): the aims of anti-homophobia education. *Sex Education* 9(2)

Allan, A, Hemingway, J, and Jennett, M (2007) No Outsiders? grappling with issues of sexual identities in group research. Paper presented at the annual meeting of the British Educational Research Association, Institute of Education, University of London 5-8 September

Apple, M (in press) On the tasks of the critical scholar/activist in education. In R Winkle-Wagner, C Hunter and D Ortloff (eds) *Bridging the Gap between Theory and Practice in Educational Research: Methods at the margins.* New York: Palgrave

Aries, P (1962) *Centuries of Childhood: A Social history of family life.* New York: Vintage.

Asthana, A (2007) The prince married a man, and lived happily ever after. *The Observer*, March 11, 2007. Retrieved 12 March 2007 from http://observer.guardian.co.uk/uk_news/story/0,,2031223,00.html

Atkinson, E (2008) Resisting compliance and rocking the boat: rekindling activism through lesbian, gay, bisexual and transgender equality work in primary schools. Paper presented at the annual Discourse, Power, Resistance conference, Manchester Metropolitan University 18-20 March

Atkinson, E and Brace, E (2007) Reinscribing 'gay': a politics of the performative in the primary school. Paper presented at the annual meeting of the British Educational Research Association, Institute of Education, University of London, 5-8 September

Atkinson, E and DePalma, R (2008a) Dangerous spaces: constructing and contesting sexual identities in an online discussion forum. *Gender and Education* 20(2), p183-194

Atkinson, E and DePalma, R (2008b) Imagining the homonormative: performative subversion in education for social justice. *British Journal of Sociology of Education* 29(1), p25-35

Atkinson, E, and DePalma, R (2009) Unbelieving the matrix: queering consensual heteronormativity. *Gender and Education* 21(1), p17-29

BBC News (1 April 2008) Anti-gay bullying books withdrawn. Retrieved 18 November, 2008 from http://news.bbc.co.uk/1/hi/england/bristol/7324985.stm

BBC Radio 4 (13 March 2007) Today Programme, 08.50 Retrieved 20 February 2009 from http://www.bbc.co.uk/radio4/today/listenagain/listenagain_20070313.shtml

Bakhtin, M (1999) *Problems of Dostoevsky's Poetics* (Vol. 8). Minneapolis: University of Minnesota Press

Barab, S, and Duffy, T (2000) From practice fields to communities of practice. In D Jonassen and S. Land (eds) *Theoretical Foundations of Learning Environments.* Englewood, NJ: Lawrence Erlbaum Associates, p25-55

Barthes, R (2005) *The Pleasure of the Text* (Trans R Miller). New York: Hill and Wang

Barton, D and Hamilton, M (2005) Literacy, reification and the dynamics of social inter-action. In D Barton and K Tusting (eds) *Beyond Communities of Practice: Language, power and social context.* Cambridge: Cambridge University Press, p14-35

Barton, D and Tusting, K (2005) Introduction. In D Barton and K Tusting (eds) *Beyond Communities of Practice: Language, power and social context,* Cambridge: Cambridge University Press, p1-13

Bass, A (1978) Translator's introduction. In J. Derrida *Writing and Difference.* Chicago: University of Chicago Press, pix-xx

Bell, D (1992) *Faces at the Bottom of the Well: The permanence of racism.* New York: Basic Books

Bell, D, Binnie, J, Cream, J and Valentine, G (1994) All hyped up and no place to go. *Gender, Place and Culture* 1(1), p31-47

Bell, D and Valentine, G (1995) *Mapping Desire, Geographies of Sexualities.* London: Routledge

Berlant, L (2004) Live sex acts (parental advisory: explicit material). In S Bruhm and N Hurley (eds) *Curiouser: On the queerness of children.* London: University of Minnesota Press, p57-80

Berry, R (2006) Inclusion, power, and community: teachers and students interpret the language of community in a inclusion classroom. *American Educational Research Journal,* 43(3), p489-529

Binnie, J (1997) Coming out of geography: towards a queer epistemology. *Environment and Planning D: Society and Space* 15(2), p223-237

Birden, S (2005) *Rethinking Sexual Identity in Education.* Lanham: Rowman and Little-field

Blaise, M (2005) *Playing it Straight: Changing images of early childhood.* London: Routledge

Bösche, S (1983) *Jenny Lives with Eric and Martin.* London: The Gay Men's Press

Brenkman, J (2002) Queer post-politics. *Narrative* 10(2), p174-180

Brettingham, M (17 October 2008) Gay Education in primaries climbs back into the closet *The Times Educational Supplement,* p20-21

Brickell, C (2000) Heroes and invaders: gay and lesbian pride parades and the public/private distinction in New Zealand media accounts. *Gender, Place and Culture* 7(2), p163-178

Britzman, D (1995) Is there a queer pedagogy? or stop reading straight. *Educational Theory* 45, p151-165

Bryson, M and de Castell, S (1993) Queer pedagogy: praxis makes im/perfect. *Canadian Journal of Education* 18 (3), p285-305

Burgess, J (2008) Radicalization and the Critique of Liberal Tolerance. *6th CHALLENGE Training School*, Paris.

Butler, J (1990) *Gender Trouble: Feminism and the subversion of identity.* London: Routledge

Butler, J (1991) Imitation and gender insubordination. In D Fuss (Ed) *Inside/Out: Lesbian theories, gay theories.* London: Routledge, p13-31

Butler, J (1993) *Bodies That Matter: On the discursive limits of 'sex.'* London: Routledge

Butler, J (1994) *Radical philosophy* 67. Accessed 5 December 2007 from www.theory.org.uk

Butler, J (1997) *Excitable Speech: A politics of the performative.* London: Routledge

Butler, J (1999a) *Gender Trouble: Feminism and the subversion of identity.* 2nd edition. London: Routledge

Butler, J (1999b) Revisiting bodies and pleasures. *Theory, Culture and Society* 16(2), p11-20

Butler, J (2004) *Undoing Gender.* London: Routledge

Butler, J (2005) *Giving an Account of Oneself.* New York: Fordham University Press

Butler, J (2007) Sexual politics: the limits of secularism, the time of coalition. *British Journal of Sociology* Public Lecture. LSE, London

Butler, J, Osborne, P, and Segal, L (1994) Gender as performance: an interview with Judith Butler. *Radical Philosophy.* 67(Summer 1994), p32-39

CLG (2007) *Discrimination Law Review: A Framework for Fairness: Proposals for a Single Equality Bill for Great Britain – A consultation paper.* London: Communities and Local Government

Campbell, A, McNamara, O and Gilroy, P (2004) *Practitioner Research and Professional Development in Education.* London: Paul Chapman

Caputo, J D (1993) *Against Ethics: Contributions to a poetics of obligation with constant reference to deconstruction.* Bloomington: Indiana University Press

Carr, W, and Kemmis, S (1986) *Becoming Critical: Education, knowledge, and action research.* London: Falmer Press

Carson, T, and Sumara, D (1997) *Action Research as a Living Practice.* New York: P. Lang

Cavanagh, S (2007) *Sexing the Teacher: School sex scandals and queer pedagogies.* Vancouver and Toronto: UBC Press

Charpentier, S (n.d.). Gender, body and the sacred: heterosexual hegemony as a sacred Order. *Queen: A Journal of Rhetoric and Power* Retrieved 21 February, 2007 from http://www.ars-rhetorica.net/Queen/Volume11/Articles/Charpentier.html

Clark, L (11 March 2007) Four-year-olds will get gay fairytales at school. *Daily Mail,* Retrieved 11 March 2007 from http://www.dailymail.co.uk/news/article-441542/Four-year-olds-gay-fairytales-school.html

Clark, L (2 April 2008) Muslims' fury forces schools to shelve anti-homophobia story-books for 5-year-olds. *Daily Mail,* Retrieved 11 December 2008 from http://www.daily mail.co.uk/news/article-553008/Muslims-fury-forces-schools-shelve-anti-homophobia-storybooks-5-year-olds.html

Clifford, J (1986) Introduction: partial truths. In G Marcus and J Clifford (eds) *Writing Culture: The poetics and politics of ethnography.* Berkeley: University of California Press, p1-27

Coffey, A and Delamont, S (2000) *Feminism and the Classroom Teacher: Research, praxis and pedagogy.* London: Routledge

Colley, H (2003) The myth of mentor as a double régime of truth: producing docility and devotion in engagement mentoring with 'disaffected' youth. In E Atkinson and J Satterthwaite (eds) *Discourse, Power, Resistance: Challenging the rhetoric of contemporary education.* Stoke on Trent: Trentham Books, p85-99

Collins, S. (2004) Ecology and ethics in participatory collaborative action research: an argument for the authentic participation of students in educational research. *Educational Action Research* 12(3), p347-362

Combs, B, Keane, D and Rappa, B (2000) *ABC: A family alphabet book.* Ridley Park PA: Two Lives Publishing

Creed, B (1995) Lesbian bodies: tribades, tomboys and tarts. In E. Grosz and E Probyn (eds) *Sexy Bodies: The strange carnalities of feminism.* London: Routledge, 86-103

Cullen, F and Sandy, L (2009) Lesbian Cinderella and other stories: telling tales and researching sexualities equalities in primary school. *Sex Education* 9(2)

Cunningham, H (2006) *The Invention of Childhood.* London: BBC Books

Davies, B (1993) *Shards of Glass: Children reading and writing beyond gendered identities.* Cresskill: Hampton Press

Davies, B, Dormer, S, Gannon, S, Laws, C. Rocco, S, Taguchi, H, *et al* (2001) Becoming schoolgirls: the ambivalent project of subjectification. *Gender and Education* 13(2), p167-182

de Certeau, M (1988) *The Practice of Everyday Life.* Berkeley: University of California Press

De Haan, L and Nijland, S (2002) *King and King.* Berkley CA: Tricycle Press

Delgado, R (1995) *The Rodrigo Chronicles: Conversations about America and race.* New York: New York University Press

DePalma, R (13-17 April, 2009). Queering gender in primary schools: exploring a trans curriculum. Paper presented at the annual meeting of the American Educational Research Association, California 13-17 April

DePalma, R (2009) Sexualities equality in all primary schools: a case for not waiting for ideal conditions. In J Koschoreck and A Tooms (eds) *Sexuality matters: Paradigms and policies for educational leaders.* Lanham: Rowman and Littlefield

DePalma, R (in press) Leaving Alinsu: towards a transformative community of practice. *Mind, Culture and Activity*

DePalma, R and Atkinson, E (2006) The sound of silence: talking about sexual orientation and schooling. *Sex Education* 6(4), p333-349

DePalma, R, and Atkinson, E (2007a) Exploring gender identity; queering heteronormativity. *International Journal of Equity and Innovation in Early Childhood* 5(7), p64-82

DePalma, R and Atkinson, E (2007b) Strategic embodiment in virtual spaces: exploring an on-line discussion about sexualities equality in schools. *Discourse: Studies in the Cultural Politics of Education* 28(4), p499-514

DePalma, R and Atkinson, E (2009) Permission to talk about it: narratives of sexuality equality in the primary classroom. *Qualitative Inquiry* 15(9), pp876-892

DePalma, R and Atkinson, E (in press) Beyond tolerance: challenging heteronormativity in primary schools through reflective action research. *British Journal of Educational Studies*

DePalma, R and Jennett, M (2007) Deconstructing heteronormativity in primary schools in England: cultural approaches to a cultural phenomenon. In L van Dijk and B van Driel (eds) *Confronting Homophobia in Educational Practice.* Stoke on Trent: Trentham

Department for Children Schools and Families (2007) *Safe to Learn: Embedding anti-bullying work in schools.* London: DCSF

Department for Education and Skills (2002) *Bullying: Don't suffer in silence.* London: DfEE

Department for Education and Skills and Department of Health (2004) *Stand up for Us: Challenging homophobia in schools.* London: DfES and DoH

Derrida, J (1974) *Of Grammatology* (Trans G Spivak). Baltimore: John Hopkins University Press

Doughty, S (16 September 2008) Teach 'the pleasure of gay sex' to children as young as five, say researchers. *Daily Mail*, Retrieved 16 September 2008 from http://www.dailymail.co.uk/news/article-1056415/Teach-pleasure-gay-sex-children-young-say-researchers.html

Edelman, L (2002) Post-partum. *Narrative* 10(2), p181-185

Edelman, L (2004) *No Future: Queer theory and the death drive.* Durham: Duke University Press

Eisenhart, M (1999) Reflections on educational intervention in light of postmodernism. *Anthropology and Educational Quarterly* 30(4), p462-465

Ellis, V (2007). Sexualities and schooling in England after Section 28: measuring and managing 'at risk' identities. *Journal of Gay and Lesbian Issues in Education* 4(3), p13-30

Ellis, C and Bochner, A (1996) *Composing Ethnography: Alternative forms of qualitative writing.* Lanham: Alta Mira

Ellis, V and High, S (2004) Something more to tell you: gay, lesbian or bisexual young people's experiences of secondary schooling. *British Educational Research Journal,* 30(2), p213-225

Engeström, Y (2007) From communities of practice to mycorrhizae. In J Hughes, N Jewson and L Unwin (eds) *Communities of Practice: Critical perspectives.* London: Routledge, p41-54

Epstein, D (1997) Cultures of schooling, cultures of sexuality. *Inclusive Education* 1(1), p37-53

Epstein, D (1999) Sex play: romantic significations, sexism and silences in the schoolyard. In D Epstein and J Sears (eds.) *A Dangerous Knowing: Sexuality, pedagogy and popular culture.* London: Cassell, p25-43

Epstein, D and Johnson, R (1998) *Schooling Sexualities.* Buckingham: Open University Press

Epstein, D, O' Flynn, S and Telford, D (2003) *Silenced Sexualities in Schools and Universities.* Stoke on Trent: Trentham

Fairclough, N (2003) *Analysing Discourse: Textual analysis for social research.* London: Routledge

Fierstein, H and Cole, H (2002) *The Sissy Duckling.* New York: Aladdin Paperbacks

Fine, M (1988) Sexuality, schooling, and adolescent females: the missing discourse of desire. *Harvard Educational Review* 58(1) p 29-53

Fine, M (1994) Working the hyphens: reinventing the Self and Other in qualitative research. In N Denzin and Y Lincoln (eds) *Handbook of Qualitative Research.* Newbury Park: Sage

Fine, M, and McClelland, S (2006) Sexuality, education and desire: still missing after all these years. *Harvard Educational Review* 76(3), p297-338

Foucault, M (1970) *The Order of Things: An archaeology of the human sciences.* London: Tavistock Publications

Foucault, M (1974) *The eye of power.* Retrieved 28 August 2007 from http://foucault. info/documents/foucault.eyeOfPower.en.html

Foucault, M (1978) *The History of Sexuality, vol. 1* (Trans. Robert Hurley). New York: Vintage

Foucault, M. (1977) *Discipline and punish: the birth of the prison* (Trans A Sheridan) London: Penguin

Foucault, M (1982) The subject and power. In H Dreyfus and P Rabinow (eds) *Michel Foucault: Beyond hermeneutics and structuralism.* Brighton: Harvester, p208-226

Foucault, M (1985) *The Use of Pleasure: The history of sexuality, vol. 2* (Trans Robert Hurley). New York: Vintage

Foucault, M (1988a) An aesthetics of existence. In L Kritzman (Ed) *Michel Foucault – Politics, Philosophy, Culture: interviews and other writings 1977-1984.* London: Routledge, p47-56

Foucault, M (1988b) Critical theory/intellectual history. In L Kritzman (Ed) *Michel Foucault – Politics, Philosophy, Culture: interviews and other writings 1977-1984*. London: Routledge, p17-46

Foucault, M (1988c) 'The return of morality. In L Kritzman (Ed) *Michel Foucault – Politics, Philosophy, Culture: interviews and other writings 1977-1984*. London: Routledge, p242-254

Foucault, M (1990a) *The Care of The Self: The history of sexuality volume 3*. London: Penguin

Foucault, M (1990b) *The History of Sexuality Volume 1: An introduction*. London: Penguin

Foucault, M (1991) *Discipline and Punish: The birth of the prison*. London: Penguin

Foucault, M (1997a) The ethics of concern of the self as a practice of freedom. In P Rabinow (Ed) *Ethics: Subjectivity and truth*. New York: New Press, p281-301

Foucault, M (1997b) *Discipline and Punish: the birth of the prison* (Trans A Sheridan). New York: Vintage Books

Foucault, M (1998) *The Will to Knowledge, the History of Sexuality*. London: Penguin

Francis, B (1998) *Power Plays: Primary school children's constructions of gender, power and adult work*. Stoke on Trent: Trentham

Frankham, J, and Howes, A (2006) Talk as action in 'collaborative action research': making and taking apart teacher/researcher relationships. *British Educational Research Journal* 32(4), 617-632.

Freeman, Elizabeth. (2007) Introduction. *GLQ: A Journal of Lesbian and Gay Studies* 13 (2-3), p159-176

Freire, P (1972) *Pedagogy of the Oppressed*. Harmondsworth: Penguin

Fuller, A (2007) Critiquing theories of learning and communities of practice. In J Hughes, N Jewson and L Unwin (eds) *Communities of Practice: Critical perspectives*. London: Routledge

Gee, J (1996) *Social Linguistics and Literacies: Ideology in discourses*. London: RoutledgeFalmer

Gordon, T and Lahelma, E (1996) 'School is like an ant's nest': spatiality and embodiment in schools. *Gender and Education* 8(3), p301-311

Grew, T (16 September 2008) Christian Institute targets homophobic bullying group, *Pink News*, Retrieved 6 January 2009 from http://www.pinknews.co.uk/news/articles/2005-9020.html

Griffin, P (1992) From hiding out to coming out: empowering lesbian and gay educators. In K Harbeck (ed) *Coming out of the Classroom Closet: Gay and lesbian students and curricula*. New York: Harrington Park Press

Grosz, E (1995) Bodies and pleasures in queer theory. In J Roof and R Wiegman (eds) *Who Can Speak? Authority and critical identity*. Urbana and Chicago: University of Illinois Press

Groundwater-Smith, S and Mockler, N (2005) Practitioner research in education: beyond celebration. Paper presented at the annual meeting of the British Educational Research Association Liverpool 15 October 2005

Guha, R and Spivak, G (1988) *Selected Subaltern Studies*. Delhi: Oxford University Press

Halberstam, J (2005) *In a Queer Time and Place: Transgender bodies, subcultural lives.* New York: New York University Press

Hand, M (2007) Should we teach homosexuality as a controversial issue? *Theory and Research in Education* 5(1) p69-86

Harvey, D (2000) *Spaces of Hope.* Edinburgh: Edinburgh University Press

Harwood, V (2006) *Diagnosing 'Disorderly' Behaviour: A critique of behaviour disorder discourse.'* London: Routledge

Henriques, J, Holloway, W, Urwin, C, Venn, C, and Walkerdine, V (2004) *Changing the Subject: Psychology, social regulation and subjectivity.* London: Routledge

Hey V (2006) The politics of performative resignification. *British Journal of Sociology of Education* 27(4) p439-459

Hildreth, P and Kimble, C (2008) Introduction and overview. In C Kimble, P Hildreth and I Bourdon (eds) *Communities of Practice: Creating learning environments for educators, vol. 1.* Charlotte: North Carolina, pxi-xvii

Holloway, D (1980) 'Homosexual relationships' – the discussion continued. In M Green, D Holloway and D Watson *The Church and Homosexuality.* London: Hodder and Stoughton

Home Office. (2008) *Guidance on Combating Transphobic Bullying in Schools.* Retrieved 15 December 2008 from http://www.gires.org.uk/transbullying.php

hooks, b (1994) *Teaching to Transgress: Education as the practice of freedom.* London: Routledge

Hubbard, P (2001) Sex zones: intimacy, citizenship and public space. *Sexualities* 4(1), p51-71

Hughes, J (2007) Lost in translation: communities of practice: the journey from academic model to practitioner tool In J Hughes, N Jewson and L Unwin (eds) *Communities of Practice: Critical perspectives.* London: Routledge

Hughes, J, Jewson, N and Unwin, L (2007a) Introduction: communities of practice: a contested concept of flux. In J Hughes, N Jewson and L Unwin (eds) *Communities of Practice: Critical perspectives.* London: Routledge

Hughes, J, Jewson, N., and Unwin, L. (2007b) Conclusion: further developments and unresolved issues. In J Hughes, N Jewson and L Unwin (eds) *Communities of Practice: Critical perspectives.* London: Routledge

Hutchins, E (1994) *Cognition in the Wild.* Cambridge: MIT Press

Ingraham, C (1994) The heterosexual imaginary: feminist sociology and theories of gender. *Sociological Theory* 12(2), p203-219

Jackson, S (1982) *Childhood and Sexuality*. London: Blackwell

Jagose, A (1996) *Queer Theory: An introduction*. New York: New York University Press

Janssen, D (2008) Re-queering queer youth development: a post-developmental approach to childhood and pedagogy. *Journal of LGBT Youth* 5(3), p74-95

Jenkins, H (1998) Introduction: childhood innocence and other modern myths. In H Jenkins (Ed) *The Children's Culture Reader*. New York: New York University Press, p1-37

Jennings, K (n.d.). A Message from the Founder and Executive Director. Retrieved 23 July, 2008 from http://www.glsen.org/cgi-bin/iowa/all/about/index.html

Jewson, N (2007) Cultivating network analysis: rethinking the concept of 'community' within 'communities of practice.' In J Hughes, N Jewson and L Unwin (eds) *Communities of Practice: Critical perspectives*. London: Routledge

Kehily, M (2002). *Sexuality, Gender and Schooling: Shifting agendas in social learning*. London: Routledge

Kehily, M and Montgomery, H (2004) Innocence and experience: a historical approach to childhood and sexuality. In M Kehily (Ed) *An Introduction to Childhood Studies*. Maidenhead: Open University Press

Kemmis, S (1993) Action research and social movement: a challenge for policy research. *Education Policy Analysis Archives*. Retrieved 23 August, 2007 from http://epaa.asu.edu/epaa/v1n1.html

Khan, U (16 September 2008) Primary schools 'should celebrate homosexuality.' *Daily Telegraph* Retrieved 16 September 2008 from http://www.telegraph.co.uk/news/newstopics/politics/education/2967796/Primary-schools-should-celebrate-homosexuality.html

Kincaid, J (1992) *Child-Loving: The erotic child and Victorian culture*. London: Routledge

Kincheloe, J (1991) *Teachers as Researchers: Qualitative inquiry as a path to empowerment*. London: Falmer Press

Kissen, R (2002) *Getting Ready for Benjamin: Preparing teachers for sexual diversity in the classroom*. Lanham: Rowman and Litlefield

Kopelson, K (2002) Dis/integrating the gay/queer Binary: 'reconstructed identity politics' for a performative pedagogy. *College English* 65(1), p17-35

Lather, P (1991) *Getting Smart: Feminist research and pedagogy with/in the postmodern*. New York: Routledge

Lather P (1993) Fertile obsession: validity after poststructuralism. *The Sociological Quarterly* 34(4) p673-693

Lave, J (1996) The practice of learning. In S Chaiklin and J Lave (eds) *Understanding Practice: Perspectives on Activity and Context*. Cambridge: Cambride University Press, p3-32

Lave, J and Wenger, E (1991) *Situated Learning: Legitimate peripheral participation*. Cambridge: Cambridge University Press

Leonardo Z (2005) *Critical Pedagogy and Race*. Oxford: Blackwell

Letts, W (1999) How to make 'boys' and 'girls' in the classroom: the heteronormative Nature of elementary-school science. In W Letts and J Sears (eds) *Queering Elementary Education: Advancing the dialogue about sexualities and schooling*. Lanham: Rowman and Littlefield

Letts, W, and Sears, J (1999) *Queering Elementary Education: Advancing the dialogue about sexualities and schooling*. Lanham: Rowman and Littlefield

Linehan, C, and McCarthy, J (2001) Reviewing the 'community of practice' metaphor: an analysis of control relations in a primary school classroom. *Mind, Culture, and Activity* 8(2), p129-147

Lisotta, C (August 12 2008) Sex toys and children make uneasy bedfellows. *The Advocate*, p16

Luke, A. (2006). How to make educational policy using Foucault and Bourdieu. Paper presented at the American Educational Research Association, San Francisco, California 7-11 April

Luke, C and Gore, J (1992) *Feminism and Critical Pedagogy*. London: Routledge

Maclure, M (2003) *Discourse in Educational and Social Research*. Buckingham: Open University Press

MacNaughton, G (2000) *Rethinking Gender in Early Childhood Education*. London: Paul Chapman

Massey, D (1994) *Space, Place and Gender*. Cambridge: Polity Press

Massey, D (2005) *For Space*. London: Sage

McDowell, L (1994) Polyphony and pedagogic authority. *Area* 26(3), p241-248

McGregor, J (2003) Making spaces: teacher workplace topologies. *Pedagogy, Culture and Society* 11(3), p353-378

McGregor, J (2004) Space, power and the classroom. *Forum* 46(1), p13-18

McInnes, D (2008) Sissy-boy melancholy and the educational possibilities of incoherence. In B Davies (Ed) *Judith Butler in Conversation: Analyzing the texts and talk of everyday life*. Abington: Routledge

McNiff, J (2002) *Action Research: Principles and practice*. London: RoutledgeFalmer

McWilliam, E (1999) *Pedagogical Pleasures*. New York: Peter Lang

Mirza, H (2008) *Race, Gender and Educational Desire: Why Black women succeed and fail*. London, Routledge

Mohanty, C (1990) On race and voice: challenges for liberal education in the 1990s. *Cultural Critique* 2, p179-208

Moje, E (2000) Changing our minds, changing our bodies: power as embodied in research relations. *International Journal of Qualitative Studies in Education* 13(1), p25-42

Moore, J (2004) Living in the basement of the ivory tower: a graduate student's perspective of participatory action research within academic institutions. *Educational Action Research* 12(1), p 145-162

Munsch, R, and Martchenko, M (1982) *The Paper Bag Princess*. London: Scholastic

Nespor, J (1997) *Tangled up in School: Politics, space, bodies and signs in the educational process*. Hillsdale: Lawrence Erlbaum

Nicks, G (17 September 2008) Outrage at gay sex lessons for kids, five. *Daily Star*, Retrieved 17th September 2008 from http://www.dailystar.co.uk/news/view/51230/

Nixon, D, and East, S (2008) Stirring it up or stirring it in? perspectives on the development of sexualities equalities in faith-based primary schools. Paper presented at the Discourse Power Resistance Conference, Manchester Metropolitan University, 18-20 March

Nixon, D and Givens, N (2004) 'Miss, you're so gay.' Queer stories from trainee teachers. *Sex Education* 4(3), p217-237

Noddings, N (1996) On community. *Educational Theory* 46(3), p245-267

O'Rourke, M (2007) Ranciere and queer theory: some further thoughts. Retrieved 12 November, 2008 from httrp://ranciere.blogspot.com/2007/12/ranciere-and-queer-theory-some-further.html, accessed 13/11/2008

Paechter, C (2001) Using poststructuralist ideas. In B Francis and C Skelton (eds) *Investigating Gender: Contemporary perspectives in education*. Buckingham: Open University Press, p41-52

Paechter, C (2004a) 'Mens sana in corpore sano': cartesian dualism and the marginalisation of sex education. *Discourse: Studies in the Cultural Politics of Education* 25(3), p309-20

Paechter, C (2004b) Power relations and staffroom spaces. *Forum* 46(1), p33-35

Parnell, P, Richardson, J and Cole, H (2005) *And Tango Makes Three*. New York: Simon & Schuster Children's Publishing

Parris, M (7 January, 2009) Of course Tintin's gay. Ask Snowy. *The Times*. Retrieved from http://entertainment.timesonline.co.uk/tol/arts_and_entertainment/books/article5461005.ece

Pascoe, C (2007) *Dude you're a Fag: Masculinity and sexuality in high school*. Berkeley: University of California Press

Patai, D (1992) Minority status and the stigma of 'surplus visibility'. *Education Digest* 57(5), p35-37

Piper, C. (2000) Historical constructions of childhood innocence: removing sexuality, in: E. Heinze (Ed.) *Of innocence and autonomy: children, sex and human rights*. Dartmouth: Ashgate)

Purkiss, D (1994) *Renaissance Women: The plays of Elizabeth Cary, the poems of Aemilia Lanyer*. London: Pickering and Chatto

Rasmussen, K (2004) Places for children, children's places. *Childhood* 11(2), p155-173

Rasmussen, ML (2001) Queering schools and dangerous knowledges: some new directions in sexualities, pedagogies and schooling. Discourse: *Studies in the Cultural Politics of Education* 22(2), p263-272

Rasmussen, ML (2004) Wounded identities, sex and pleasure: 'doing it' at school. NOT! Discourse: *Studies in the Cultural Politics of Education* 25(4) p445-458

Rasmussen, ML (2006) Play School, melancholia, and the politics of recognition. *British Journal of Sociology of Education* 27(4), p473-487

Rasmussen, ML and Harwood, V (2003) Performativity, youth and injurious speech. *Teaching Education* 14(1) p25-36

Rasmussen, M, Rofes, E, and Talburt, S (2004) *Youth and Sexualities: pleasure, subversion, and insubordination in and out of school.* Basingstoke: Palgrave Macmillan

Rennert, A (2004) *We Do: A celebration of gay and lesbian marriage.* San Francisco: Chronicle Books

Renold, E (2002) Presumed innocence: heterosexual, heterosexist and homophobic harassment among primary school girls and boys. *Childhood* 9(4) p415-434

Renold, E (2005) *Girls, Boys and Junior Sexualities: Exploring children's gender and sexual relations in the primary school.* London: RoutledgeFalmer

Renold, E (2006) 'They won't let us play ... unless you're going out with one of them': girls, boys and Butler's heterosexual matrix n the primary years. *British Journal of Sociology of Education* 27(4) p489-510

Rock, F (2005) 'I've picked some up from a colleague': language, sharing and communities of practice in an institutional setting. In D. Barton and K. Tusting (eds) *Beyond Communities of Practice: Language, power and social context.* New York: Cambridge University Press

Rofes, E (2000) Bound and gagged: sexual silences, gender conformity and the gay male teacher. *Sexualities* 3(4) p439-462

Rose, G (2002) *Family Photographs and Domestic Spacings: A case study.* Milton Keynes: Open University Press

Roth, WM, Lawless, D, and Tobin, K (2000) Cogenerative dialoguing as praxis of dialectic method. *Forum Qualitative Sozialforschung/Forum: Qualitative Social Research.* Retrieved 17 October 2007 from http://www.qualitative-research.net/index.php/fqs/article/viewArticle/1054

Schwier, R and Daniel, B (2008) Implications of a virtual community model for designing distributed communities of practice in higher education. In C Kimble, P Hildreth and I Bourdon (eds) *Communities of Practice: Creating learning environments for educators, vol. 1.* Charlotte: North Carolina, p347-366

Sears, J 1998) A generation and theoretical analysis of culture and male (homo) sexuality. In W Pinar (Ed) *Queer Theory in Education.* Mahwah: Lawrence Erlbaum

Sears, J (1999) Teaching queerly: some elementary positions. In W Letts and J Sears (eds) *Queering Elementary Education: Advancing the dialogue about sexualities and schooling.* Lanham: Rowman and Littlefield

Sedgwick, E (1993) The epistemology of the closet. In H Abelove, M A Barale and D Halperin (eds) *The Lesbian and Gay Studies Reader.* London: Routledge

Serano, J (2007) *Whipping girl: A transsexual woman on sexism and the scapegoating of femininity*. Emeryville: Seal Press

Shilling, C (1991) Social space, gender inequalities and educational differentiation. *British Journal of Sociology of Education* 12(1) p23-44

Siddique, F (8 April 2008) How much do children really need to know? Bristol Evening Post Retrieved 18 November 2008 from http://www.thisisbristol.co.uk/display Node.jsp?nodeId=144913&command=displayContent&sourceNode=221367&conten tPK=20343266&folderPk=103578&pNodeId=221369

Silin, J (1995) *Sex, Death, and the Education of Children: Our passion for ignorance in the age of AIDS*. New York: Teachers College Press

Silverstein, C and Picano, F (1993) *The New Joy of Gay Sex*. London: GMP

Skeggs, B (1999) Matter out of place: visibility, violence and movement in the city. *Leisure Studies* 18, p213-232

Slee, R (1995) *Changing Theories and Practices of Discipline*. London: Falmer

Sorkin Rabinowitz, N (2002) Queer theory and feminist pedagogy. In A Macdonald and S Sanchez-Casal (eds) *Twenty First Century Feminist Classrooms*. New York: Palgrave Macmillan

Spivak, G (1988) Subaltern studies: deconstructing historiography. In R Guha and G Spivak (eds) *Selected Subaltern Studies*. Oxford: Oxford University Press

Smith, A (1994) *New Right Discourse on Race and Sexuality: Britain, 1968-1990*. Cambridge: Cambridge University Press

Smith, M (1994) *Local Education: Community, conversation, praxis*. Buckingham: Open University Press

Somekh, B (2002) Inhabiting each others' castles: toward knowledge and mutual growth through collaboration. In C Day, J Elliott, B.Somekh and R Winter (eds) *Theory and Practice in Action Research: Some international perspectives*

Somekh, B (2005). Transforming professional knowledge through a global action research community. Paper presented at the First Congress for Qualitative Inquiry, University of Illinois 5-7 May

Somekh, B (2006) The nature of teachers' action research in the evaluation in England of an innovative program of school reform through the use of technology. Paper presented at the annual meeting of the American Educational Research Association, San Francisco 7-11 April

Somekh, B (2006) Action research: *A methodology for change and development*. Maidenhead: Open University Press

Spivak, G (1988) Subaltern studies: deconstructing historiography. In R Guha and G Spivak (eds) *Selected Subaltern Studies*. Oxford: Oxford University Press

St. Pierre, E (1997) An introduction to figurations – a poststructural practice of inquiry. *Qualitative Studies in Education* 10(3), p279-284

St. Pierre, E and Pillow, W (2000) *Working the Ruins: Feminist poststructural theory and methods in education*. London: Routledge

Stanley, J, and Wise, S (1993) *Breaking Out Again: Feminist ontology and episte-mology.* London: Routledge

Sullivan, N (1999) Queer pleasures: some thoughts. *Social Semiotics* 9(2) p251-255

Sumara, D and Davis, B (1999) Interrupting heteronormativity: towards a queer curriculum theory. *Curriculum Inquiry* 29(2) p191-208

Talburt, S and Steinberg, S (2000) *Thinking Queer: Sexuality, culture, and education.* New York: Peter Lang

Thorne, B (1993) *Gender Play: Boys and girls in school.* New Jersey: Rutgers University Press

Tobin, J (1997) Introduction: the missing discourse of pleasure and desire. In J Tobin (Ed) *Making a Place for Pleasure in Early Childhood Education.* New Haven: Yale University Press

Tusting, K (2005) Language and power in communities of practice. In D Barton and K Tusting (eds) *Beyond communities of practice: Language, power and social context.* Cambridge: Cambridge University Press

Valentine, G (1996) (Re)negotiating the 'heterosexual street': lesbian productions of space. In N Duncan (Ed) *Bodyspace: Destabilizing geographies of gender and sexuality.* London: Routledge

Walkerdine, V (1998) *Counting Girls Out: Girls and mathematics.* London: Falmer Press

Wardrop, M (27 February 2009) Gay 'Romeo and Julian' school play sparks political correctness debate. *Daily Telegraph* Retrieved 8 March 2009 from http://www.telegraph.co.uk/education/educationnews/4842414/Gay-Romeo-and-Julian-school-play-sparks-political-correctness-debate.html

Warner, M (1976) *Alone of All Her Sex: The myth and cult of the Virgin Mary.* London: Weidenfeld and Nicolson

Weiner, G (1994) *Feminisms and Education.* Buckingham: Open University Press

Wenger, E (1998) *Communities of Practice: Learning, meaning and identity.* Cambridge: Cambridge University Press

Wenger, E, McDermott, R and Snyder, W (2002) *Cultivating Communities of Practice.* Boston: Harvard Business School Press

Westlander, G (2006) Researcher roles in action research. In K Nielson and L Svensson (eds) *Action and Interactive Research: Beyond practice and theory.* Maastricht, Netherlands: Shaker Publishing

Whyte, W (1991) *Participatory Action Research.* Newbury Park: Sage Publications

Winkelmann, C (1991) Social acts and social systems: community as metaphor. *Linguistics and Education* 3(1), p1-29

Youdell, D (2003) Identity traps or how Black students fail : the interactions between biographical, sub-cultural, and learner identities. *British Journal of Sociology of Education* 24(1), p3-20

Youdell, D (2004a) Wounds and reinscriptions: schools, sexualities and performative subjects. *Discourse* 25(4) p477-494

Youdell, D (2004b) Bent as a ballet dancer: the possibilities and limits for a legitimate homosexuality in school. In ML Rasmussen, E Rofes and S Talburt (eds) *Youth and Sexualities: Pleasure, subversion and insubordination in and out of schools.* Basingstoke: Palgrave, p 201-222

Youdell, D (2005) Sex-gender-sexuality: how sex, gender and sexuality constellations are constituted in secondary schools. *Gender and Education* 17(3) p149-170

Youdell, D (2006a) *Impossible Bodies, Impossible Selves: Exclusions and student subjectivities.* Dordrecht: Springer

Youdell, D (2006b) Diversity, inequality, and a post-structural politics for education. *Discourse* 27(1) p33-42

Youdell, D. (2007) Queer classrooms? The possibilities for post-structural pedagogies in primary classrooms or lessons in praxis: things I need to remember about power/knowledge, subjectivity and politics. Paper presented at the annual meeting of the British Educational Research Association, Institute of Education, University of London 5-8 September

Index